Women Champions of Human Rights

In memory of my mother,
Marjorie Bolton Davison

Women Champions of Human Rights

Eleven U.S. Leaders of the Twentieth Century

by

Moira Davison Reynolds

McFarland & Company, Inc., Publishers
Jefferson, North Carolina, and London

I contend that woman has as much
right. . . as man. . . to sit in the presidential
chair of the United States. . . .

—Angelina Grimké, 1838

British Library Cataloguing-in-Publication data are available

Library of Congress Cataloguing-in-Publication Data

Reynolds, Moira Davison.
  Women champions of human rights : eleven U.S. leaders of the
twentieth century / by Moira Davison Reynolds.
      p.   cm.
  Includes bibliographical references and index.
  ISBN 0-89950-614-3 (lib. bind. : 55# alk. paper) ∞
  1. Women social reformers—United States—Biography.
2. Feminists—United States—Biography.   3. Women's rights—United
States—History—20th century.   4. Women—United States—Social
conditions.   I. Title.
HQ1412.R497   1991
973'.0992—dc20
  [B]   91-52505
                                                                                CIP

Printed in the United States of America

McFarland & Company, Inc., Publishers
  Box 611, Jefferson, North Carolina 28640

Contents

Illustrations

Preface and Acknowledgments

This book evolved from my *Nine American Women of the Nineteenth Century: Leaders into the Twentieth*. The subjects of both books are selected American women and their enduring monuments. However, I have added a criterion for the current book: at least 25 years must have elapsed since the woman's significant work. I considered many subjects, and the selection reflects my bias and interests.

Women Champions is intended for the general reader who is interested in American history. Professional historians will find nothing new, but what is familiar to them is often new to the laity.

As usual, I am much indebted to three libraries: Marquette's Peter White Public Library, Northern Michigan University's Lydia M. Olson Library, and Superiorland Library Cooperative. Joanne Whitley of the latter has been my mainstay in locating hard-to-find materials.

I am indebted to Mrs. Maryjean McKelvy of *Action Shopper News* for excellent proofreading.

My special thanks goes to Mrs. Margaret Whitman who has a long-standing interest in women's history for reading the manuscript and adding her corrections.

Moira Davison Reynolds
Marquette, Michigan

vii

Introduction

The nineteenth century was coming to a close when Jane Addams opened Hull House to the immigrants of its Chicago neighborhood. When Hull House celebrated its centenary one hundred years later, Addams was regarded as the foremost social worker of the twentieth century.

Close to the time of the opening of Hull House, a Bostonian named Fannie Farmer wrote a cookbook with field-tested recipes that stressed *level* measurements, an innovation at the time. That cookbook gained popularity with each succeeding edition during Farmer's lifetime. After her death, there were revised editions; one is still in print, as is a facsimile of the 1896 edition. And careful measurement is, of course, accepted as part of good cooking.

Lillian Wald, a young Jewish woman, began in 1893 to provide visiting nurse services to the immigrants living in the crowded and squalid tenements of New York's Lower East Side. As more and more newcomers reached these shores, Wald extended the services, in the process creating the school nurse program. Today, Lillian Wald is considered a significant figure in the evolution of American public health.

The year that Wald's Henry Street Settlement was trying a pilot project with a school nurse, Mary McLeod Bethune founded a school in Florida for black girls. The daughter of illiterate slaves, Bethune realized the value of an education; as a black woman she had experienced firsthand the injustice and roadblocks imposed in the South. Her school became an accredited coeducational college. Her reputation as an educator led her to an appointment by President Franklin Roosevelt as director of the Division of Negro Affairs of the National Youth Administration. She devoted her life to the cause of racial equality.

In 1912, in Savannah, Georgia, a Southerner named Juliette Low formed the first troop of Girl Guides in the United States. The current membership of Girl Scouts of the U.S.A. exceeds three million.

The same year, a Henry Street nurse named Margaret Sanger gave up maternity work to devote herself to the cause of birth control. Spurred by the misery she attributed to unwanted pregnancy, Sanger opened the nation's first birth-control clinic in 1917. A sequence of 30 days in the workhouse failed to deter her efforts. She founded the organization now called the Planned Parenthood Federation of America (there are some 170 affiliates throughout the nation) and lived to see the removal of restrictive laws governing the availability of birth-control services and information.

During the nineteenth century, many women had worked hard, but without complete success, for the right to vote. The final victory, the Nineteenth Amendment to the Constitution in 1920, is a monument to the political strategy at both state and federal levels of Carrie Chapman Catt. Catt was also the prime mover in setting up the League of Women Voters, an organization that still provides nonpartisan education information about political issues and candidates.

Reading provided escape from the harsh realities of the depression years. Perhaps this contributed to the success of Margaret Mitchell's 1936 novel, *Gone with the Wind.* A record breaker for sales, it was also awarded a Pulitzer Prize. Blacks did not agree with its portrayal of slaves, but it ranked Mitchell as a superb storyteller.

Margaret Bourke-White's photographs, taken over two decades in many parts of the world, remain as a memorial to her ability as a photographer and a journalist. In 1942, Bourke-White became the first woman to be accredited as a war correspondent to the United States Army.

The country recovered from World War II, became involved in the cold war, and turned its attention to the environment. Largely responsible for this new interest was biologist-author Rachel Carson, who wrote *Silent Spring* in 1962. In this book Carson warned that chemical pesticides and herbicides could upset the world's natural ecological balance.

A year after *Silent Spring*, Betty Friedan's *The Feminine Mystique* appeared. Friedan contended that a woman's role as wife and mother restricted her fulfillment unless she also had creative, self-defining work. In 1966, Friedan founded the National Organization for Women, a civil-rights group dedicated to equality of opportunity for women. Thus she is largely responsible for today's women's movement.

These eleven women represent a variety of viewpoints and motives. Some were more influential than others; some worked assiduously for or supported causes with limited success, among them peace, the ERA, and Prohibition. Yet each of these women left her stamp on the twentieth century. In the pages ahead you may read how their efforts turned some of their dreams and ambitions into reality.

Jane Addams

During the closing years of the nineteenth century, Chicago became the new home of thousands of European immigrants. Many had agrarian backgrounds and soon found that skills useful on the farm were not needed in the city. Isolated from familiar support systems of relatives and friends, understanding little English, and facing an alien culture given to exploiting them, they often led lives of misery and hopelessness. Hull House, a social settlement founded in 1889, became a light in their darkness and in the darkness of millions more who reached these shores in the early 1900s. The woman behind Hull House was Jane Addams, and this is her story.

Her father was John H. Addams. He had originally been a miller in Pennsylvania but later settled in rural Illinois where he purchased a sawmill with money from his father. He added a gristmill, worked hard, prospered, and soon was making enough money to allow him to invest some of it. A public-spirited man, he helped to organize the first church and school in Cedarville, the town that had grown up in the area where he had settled. Addams was an avid reader, so it was not surprising that Cedarville's first subscription library was run from his home. He was also instrumental in starting the Galena and Chicago Union Railway. Serving as a Republican state senator from 1854–1870, he was noted for his integrity. He knew Lincoln in the senate and remained steadfast in his support of him. During the Civil War, Addams raised a regiment for Illinois. He died at 49, a rich and highly respected man. Jane was devoted to him and believed that he played a dominant part in her thinking.

Addams's first wife was Sarah Weber, whom he knew in Pennsylvania. She came from a prosperous family and had been sent to boarding school in Philadelphia. She died having her ninth child. Her eighth was Jane Addams, born on September 6, 1860. Since Jane was 2½ when her biological mother died, Sarah's influence could not have been significant. Anna Haldeman Addams, a widow, became Jane's stepmother in 1888, and the two appeared to have a good relationship during Jane's girlhood. Later on, there was bitterness between them, possibly because Mrs. Addams was not enthusiastic about giving her husband's money to Hull House. Anna's good taste, appreciation of culture, and her husband's money insured that Jane, or "Jennie" as she was then called, grew up in a comfortable home. Nevertheless, she attended a one-room school and lived in a rural atmosphere. Her constant companion between 8 and 17 was George Haldeman, her stepbrother. Later he wanted to marry her, but Jane seemed bent on a different life and remained single.

Some young women of her generation were beginning to attend college. Jane wanted to obtain a bachelor's degree from Smith College in Northampton, Massachusetts. Yielding to pressure from her father to attend nearby Rockford Female Seminary, where he was a trustee, she enrolled there when she was 17. (Rockford, known as the Mount Holyoke of the West, had not yet granted a degree, but after receiving a seminary certificate in 1882, Jane returned the following year to the newly named Rockford College to receive a B.A. degree.) As at Mount Holyoke, acknowledgment of Christ as one's personal savior was encouraged. Jane, like her father, belonged to no organized religion, and throughout her years at Rockford remained unmoved by calculated evangelical appeal. She did enjoy the intellectual stimulation, studying Latin, Greek, natural science, ancient history, literature, mental and moral philosophy, French, and calculus. She also concentrated her efforts on developing skill in English composition. It was during her college days that she became acquainted with Ellen Gates Starr, with whom she would found Hull House.

Some of her public utterances as a student at Rockford presaged her professional life: "Believing that labor alone is happiness, and that the only true and honorable life is one filled with good works and honest toil, we will strive to idealize our labor and thus happily fulfill woman's noblest mission." And in an essay she suggested that women must gain what the ancients referred to as the right of speakers to make themselves heard. She also wrote, "All that subtle force among women which is now dream fancy, might be changed into creative genius."

John Addams died suddenly in 1881, and the fall of that year saw Jane enrolled at the Women's Medical College of Philadelphia. She did not care for the curriculum and quit after a few months. Whether she was physically or mentally ill is not clear. She did have some sort of a back ailment that was considered serious enough to be treated surgically. Large numbers of women in the Victorian era suffered from vague illnesses; whether such disorders were imaginary or otherwise is usually difficult to determine in retrospect.

Jane was sufficiently recovered to tour Europe from August 1883 until June 1885. Accompanying her were Anna, two friends from Rockford College, and their aunt, as well as a Rockford teacher. Jane kept careful records of this European adventure. She read books on art, history, and the like, and studied German, Italian, and French.

The Addamses spent the winter of 1885 in Baltimore where George Haldeman was studying at Johns Hopkins University and where his mother was seeking a better social life than that provided by Cedarville. Jane, however, "reached the nadir of . . . nervous depression and sense of maladjustment."

In 1887, she began a second trip to Europe. This time, her friend Ellen Starr joined her in Germany. Ellen had left Rockford after just one year. She had taught art appreciation and English, at first in a small Illinois town, then at the Kirkland School for Girls in Chicago. In the intervening years, she and Jane had kept in contact.

In London, Jane was interested in the new People's Palace that made meeting rooms, workshops and clubrooms available to the working poor. Toynbee Hall, the pioneer social settlement, impressed her. It was named in honor of Arnold Toynbee (1852–1883), the social reformer and Oxford economist who had worked for the poor of the Whitechapel district. She had read Walter Besant's *Children of Gibeon* and *All Sorts and Conditions of Men*, both of which also focused her thoughts on the poor.

On her return to Cedarville in 1888, Jane was baptized as a Presbyterian and joined that church. Religion played a small role in her life during the early years of Hull House; later it appeared to have little or no significance.

At 28, Jane Addams had a good education, enriched through travel and study; she had sufficient income ($3,000 a year) to preclude her working; she was a dutiful daughter and a loving aunt; but she had no real purpose in life.

A vague plan had been developing in her mind, very likely stimulated by her recent visit to Toynbee Hall. She and Ellen would live in the Chicago slums, "next door to poverty," and they and their neighbors would learn from and help one another. She was now convinced that "dependence of classes on each other is reciprocal."

By 1889, the two women and a housekeeper had moved into a once-elegant brick mansion built in 1856 by Charles J. Hull, a real-estate developer. It was located at Polk and Halsted streets between an undertaking establishment and a saloon. Jane and Ellen sublet the second floor and arranged to use a large reception room on the first floor. They felt confident that they could interest other women like themselves in instructing and working at the residence-settlement, which would be known as Hull House (sometimes hyphenated). About the type of woman they envisaged as a prospective colleague, Jane wrote, "[In the first year after leaving school], she does not understand this apparent waste of herself, this elaborate preparation, if no work is provided for her." So in Jane's mind, the reciprocity included self-fulfillment as well as a broadened viewpoint for the middle- or upper-class woman. Sociologists have pointed out that college-educated

Jane Addams (circa 1889). Courtesy Rockford College Archives.

women of the era often had little desire to live at home after graduation, and the settlement house offered them an attractive option.

Toynbee Hall had evolved largely from the ideas of Oxford idealist philosopher Thomas Hill Green, John Ruskin, and Arnold Toynbee himself. Following their principles, Samuel August Barnett, an Anglican vicar, founded it by inviting university students to join him and Mrs.

Barnett (Henrietta Rowland) in "settling" in a deprived area of London.

An American visitor to Toynbee Hall, Stanton Coit, started the first social settlement in the United States in 1887, New York's Neighborhood Guild, later known as University Settlement. Its central feature was the club, and by 1889, membership in clubs had reached 147 (girls and boys). Hull House just missed being the second settlement. Earlier in 1889, the College Settlement Association, composed of representatives of some women's colleges, had opened the College Settlement, again in New York City. Two years after Hull House settlement came into existence, William Tucker and Robert Woods, the latter yet another American who had lived at Toynbee Hall, started Andover House, which in turn became Boston's well-known South End House. By this time, the settlement movement was spreading rapidly both nationally and internationally. In this country, the period of great influence of the settlements lasted from 1890 until 1910. By the latter date, there were more than 400.

This rise of the settlement movement corresponded roughly with the mass European immigration that peaked in 1907 when some 1.3 million foreigners arrived here. Most of these immigrants sought cities, New York in particular. However, Chicago had its share. In 1889, the Windy City had a total population of about 1 million, three-quarters of whom were born abroad. Italians, Irish, and Germans predominated in the neighborhood of Hull House; there were also many German, Polish, and Russian Jews.

The country's second most populous city was considered progressive and energetic. In just four years, its spectacular Columbian Exposition (World's Fair) would be lit with electricity. There were money and power in class-conscious Chicago, but not in the hands of the majority immigrants. Influence lay with a small minority of American families—the Armours, Fields, McNallys, Pullmans, Woolworths, and so on. There were jobs, but the wages were poor. Of course, health and unemployment benefits did not exist, and Social Security was yet to come.

Three years before the opening of Hull House, 80,000 workers were striking on behalf of an eight-hour day. When one of the strikers was killed at the McCormick Harvesting Machine Company, anarchists called a protest meeting at Haymarket Square. An unknown person hurled a bomb into the crowd, killing seven policemen who had been trying to break up the gathering. It was never legally proved that the Knights of Labor were implicated, but the incident served to stamp that union and the eight-hour day with the marks of violence and subversion.

Having secured a place to "settle," Jane and Ellen focused on obtaining financial support and the assistance of women of leisure who would give time and talent to the new project. Jane, who was now a church member and considered the undertaking part of Christian benevolence, spoke to representatives of various religious faiths. Their plans were also presented to the Philanthropy Committee of the Chicago Woman's Club, the local branch of the Association of Collegiate Alumnae (now American Association of University Women), and similar groups.

Ellen, who came from an affluent family, did her part. Her connection with the Kirkland School brought many socially prominent young women to Hull House to become club leaders, instruct classes, and so on.

Jane told the socially prominent that the settlement would help "Germans and Bohemians and Italians and Poles and Russians and Greeks in Chicago vainly trying to adjust their peasant habits to the life of a large city." She did not neglect to emphasize the reciprocity idea and used the British experience: "Toynbee Hall was first projected as an aid and outlet to educated young men," she said. "The benefit to East Londoners was then regarded as almost secondary, and the benefit has always been held as strictly mutual." From the beginning, she was successful in obtaining the necessary support and interest, and she continued to do this throughout her career.

Ellen had considerable knowledge of art; in keeping with settlement philosophy, she and Jane were resolved to share this with their new neighbors. (John Ruskin had gone so far as to advocate that men should find "pleasure in the work by which they make their bread.") As time went by, Hull House became known for its objects of art and elegant appointments. Determined to provide an attractive and homelike atmosphere, Jane even made available items of her own, such as the silver she had inherited. Literature too was to be shared, and their first venture was to invite some Italians to a reading in Italian of George Eliot's *Ramola*. Slides of Florentine art were shown at the same gathering.

Hull House's charter stated its purpose and, it turned out, the sequence of events that followed its beginning: "To provide a center for a higher civic and social life; to institute and maintain educational and philanthropic enterprises, and to investigate and improve the conditions in the industrial districts of Chicago." The Hull House residents who improved conditions in Chicago at the end of the 1800s spurred twentieth-century reforms in Illinois and the nation.

As the number of residents grew, so did the activities. The wealthy increased their donations, thanks to Jane's efforts, and by 1907, the settlement had become a complex of 13 buildings that included an art gallery, gymnasium, theater, dining hall, and apartments for the staff. Kindergarten and day-care facilities for children of working mothers, an employment bureau, various clubs, music and art classes, and meeting places for groups such as trade unions were provided. Helen Culver, niece of the owner of the Hull mansion, soon donated that building and some adjacent property to the settlement organization that was named Hull House Association.

Hull House neighborhood about 1892. (Courtesy of Jane Addams Memorial Collection, Special Collections, The University Library, University of Illinois at Chicago.)

To gain some understanding of how Jane Addams became involved in such a variety of reform activities, we shall take a look at some of the problems she encountered in the neighborhood soon after her arrival. A few of those she recounted in her 1912 book *Twenty Years at Hull-House* are presented here.

"Fallen" women had to be dealt with when two young girls who had been prostitutes came directly from the obstetrical ward to Hull House, infants in their arms. They were afraid of "being licked" if they returned to their families.

On witnessing the fright of an old woman about to be removed from her home to the county poorhouse, Jane sensed that this must be the dread of many others.

The inadequacy of the immigrant poor to deal with the bureaucracy was soon apparent to her. She wrote:

> We early found ourselves spending many hours in efforts to secure support for deserted women, insurance for bewildered widows, damages for injured operators, furniture from the clutches of the installment store. The Settlement is valuable as an information and interpretation bureau. It constantly acts between the various institutions of the city and the people for whose benefit these institutions were erected. The hospitals, the county agencies, and State asylums are often but vague rumors to the people who need them most.

Christmas 1889 taught Jane something about child labor: "A number of little girls refused the candy which was offered them as part of the Christmas cheer, saying simply that they 'worked in a candy factory and could not bear the sight of it.' We discovered that for six weeks they had worked from seven in the morning until nine at night, and that they were exhausted as well as satiated."

Jane quickly recognized that Chicago's resources did not come close to serving the needs of its poor.

> The lack of municipal regulation already referred to was, in the early days of Hull House, paralleled by the inadequacy of the charitable efforts of the city and an unfounded optimism that there was no real poverty among us. Twenty years ago there was no Charity Organization in Chicago and the Visiting Nurse Association had not yet begun its beneficent work, while the relief societies, although conscientiously administered, were inadequate in extent and antiquated in method.

Ironically, charity was for many years often scorned when offered. This is illustrated by Jane's account of a dying Scottish woman's last words:

> So you came in yourself this morning, did you? You only sent things yesterday. I guess you knew when the doctor was coming. Don't try to warm my feet with anything but that old jacket that I've got there; it belonged to my boy who was drowned at sea nigh thirty years ago, but it's warmer yet with human feelings than any of your damned charity hot-water bottles.

Obviously, the problems were numerous. With Jane as the prime mover, they were attacked in the years to come. Solutions come from people, and Hull House was fortunate in attracting many outstanding individuals. One of these early residents was Florence Kelley. A graduate of

Cornell University, she studied in Europe and embraced socialism (she translated into English one of Friedrich Engel's books). After returning to the United States, she resided in Illinois with the hope of winning a divorce under that state's laws. At Hull House she began her lifelong work on behalf of labor legislation.

In 1892, she investigated tenement sweatshops of the garment industry for the Illinois Bureau of Labor Statistics. Here is an example of the conditions she found: "I spent seven hours yesterday in a district where smallpox is epidemic. I found clothing manufactured in houses where there were smallpox patients. . . . I spent three hours looking for a coat which had been made in a room with a smallpox patient and at last found it hidden in a house where four cases of smallpox had developed since the coat had been secreted there." Her findings did much to prompt an 1893 Illinois law to limit working hours for women and to regulate tenement sweatshops and child labor. Governor John Peter Altgeld and Hull House residents campaigned to push through the law. Two years later, the Illinois Supreme Court declared the eight-hour provision unconstitutional, but its passage showed what determined settlement workers could accomplish.

The 1893 law provided for a chief factory inspector with staff, and the governor appointed Florence Kelley to the post. She proved to be very effective in exposing violations of the laws. She also enrolled as a law student at Northwestern University, graduating in 1894. A new governor terminated her position in 1897. Two years later, she moved to New York City to organize consumers to promote higher wages and better working conditions for workers. She became a resident of Henry Street Settlement, as we shall see in the chapter on Lillian Wald. Her efforts helped to create the Children's Bureau in 1912.

Kelley was associated with minimum-wage legislation in several states and with passage of a federal child-labor law in 1916. Although these acts were later overturned by the Supreme Court, the principles she fought for were reflected in what eventually became the laws of the land.

Florence Kelley had spearheaded a project that produced *Hull-House Maps and Papers*, published in 1895. The book was based on facts obtained by the residents when they made a systematic survey that focused on the nationality and income of their neighbors. Reports of this type turned Jane's interest to social reform. Under Florence's influence, she came to consider this more important in the life of immigrants than the role of art. Until her death in 1932, Florence Kelley remained a friend and admirer of Jane Addams.

Another early resident who attained fame was Julia Lathrop. Ten years after graduating from Vassar, she joined Hull House in 1890. Appointed by Governor Altgeld to the Illinois Board of Charities, she personally made inspections of county almshouses and farms in the state. One winter she concentrated on charity institutions in Cook County, where Chicago is located. She had studied law and actively worked with Jane and others for a juvenile court system in Chicago. (In 1899, Cook County Juvenile Court, the first of its kind, came into being.) On the national scene, Lathrop was the first head of the Children's Bureau. Appointed by President Taft in 1912, she served until 1921. Toward the end of her life, she was an assessor for the Child Welfare Committee of the League of Nations.

Lathrop's Chicago experiences convinced her of the importance of formal training for persons who staff public institutions. Around 1904, she helped to organize the Chicago Institute of Social Science, later renamed the Chicago School of Civics and Philanthropy. She was associated with this institution, some of the time as a trustee, until in 1920 it became the School of Social Service Administration of the University of Chicago.

Hull House's growing prominence ensured the continuing presence of competent and dedicated residents. From almost the beginning, there were male as well as female residents. Resident Alice Hamilton arrived in 1897 after obtaining an M.D. from the University of Michigan. Work done with a state commission prompted her pioneer studies, around 1912, of lead poisoning among pottery workers and painters. For the next 30 years she studied occupational disease and was considered an authority on the subject. She lived at Hull House for only a few years but maintained contact for many.

The Abbott sisters, Grace and Edith, came to Hull House in the first decade of the new century. Grace had academic connections with the University of Chicago. She studied immigration, publishing books on the subject. In 1921, President Harding named her successor to Julia Lathrop as head of the Children's Bureau. In 1924 Edith became dean of the School of Social Science Administration at the University of Chicago. In 1910, she wrote *Women in Industry* and in 1936 *The Tenements of Chicago*.

A close associate of the Abbotts was Sophonisba Breckinridge, a lawyer. She was a champion of labor legislation and a supporter of women's trade unions. She also worked for the practical training of social workers since professionally trained social workers were a new breed.

These women were more or less privileged. Certainly as a group they had more formal education than most of their female contemporaries. One resident with a different background was Mary Kenney O'Sullivan. Born in Missouri and having only a few years of schooling, she came to Chicago in 1889. Working in various bookbinderies goaded her determination to improve the lot of workers. She succeeded in organizing Chicago's women bookbinders as part of the American Federation of Labor. Jane opened Hull House to these workers, and enduring bonds between Mary Kenney (she was then unmarried) and Jane, Mary Lathrop, and Florence Lathrop were formed. One of Jane's biographers. Allen Davis, has pointed out that Mary Kenney influenced Jane's thinking about unions.

Because of the dedication of scores of persons encouraged or led by Jane, Hull House's firsts are impressive. For Chicago, these include the first public bath, first college extension course, first fresh-air school, and first swimming pool. Chicago's first probation officer was a Hull House resident named Alzina Stevens. Florence Kelley, Julia Lathrop, and others made Hull House known in Illinois and beyond. Jane was responsible for most of its fame. That Hull House's reputation had spread beyond Halsted Street is evident from Jane's writing: "By 1909 ... we had already discovered that our intellectual interests, our convictions and activities were all becoming parts of larger movements and that research into social conditions was gradually being developed in the universities and by the great foundations." So the principles that Hull House Association stood for were the foundation of professional social work in the United States.

An interesting comment on this professionalism appeared in the introduction by Harvey Wish, a history professor, to the 1964 edition of William T. Stead's famous 1895 book, *If Christ Came to Chicago*. Professor Wish wrote:

> In the eager Peace Corps youth there is more than a suggestion of the enthusiastic college men and women of the Nineties who chose to share the life of the slums, not as a gesture of condescension but to provide much-needed leadership that was usually missing in neighborhoods of great poverty ... the disciples of Jane Addams and Hull House continue to win new victories for social security and the preservation of the family, while the adherents of the old Social Gospel still seek to build a kingdom of righteousness on earth; the idealists, however, with this historical perspective complain that modern professionalism, as in social work, has left a serious vacuum for the vital amateur or volunteer spirit.

There was and would continue to be a constant stream of visitors from all walks of life, representing a variety of views. Here are the names of a few: John Dewey, Clarence Darrow, Theodore Roosevelt, Amelia Earhart, Eleanor Roosevelt. A famous alumnus of the music school was Benny Goodman.

It was Jane's wisdom, her personality, character, and insight, that accounted for much of Hull House's remarkable success. Since her neighborhood was home to so many immigrants, much of Jane's efforts involved them. She was able to ferret out seemingly unimportant facts, facts that she could often use to make their lives more bearable. She wrote of "the curious isolation of many of the immigrants" and gave an example of an Italian woman who had never dreamed of sallying forth from her home to visit even a public park. She noted the tyranny imposed by immigrant parents, "who, eager for money and accustomed to the patriarchal authority of peasant households, hold their children in a stern bondage which requires surrender of all their wages and concedes no time or money for pleasures."

Other settlements worked with foreigners, but their approach was different: greater emphasis was placed on learning the English language and gaining some familiarity with American history and the structure of our government. In other words, measures that would hasten the attainment of American citizenship were stressed. The melting-pot concept was paramount.

Hull House always respected alien cultures. In Jane's words, it aimed "to preserve and keep whatever of value [the immigrants'] past life contained." It was not until after World War II that the idea of cultural pluralism was encouraged, so Jane was ahead of her time about this.

Hull House could assist in more tangible ways too. Writing about the exploitation of foreigners, she observed:

> The sturdy peasants eager for work were either the victims of the padrone who fleeced them unmercifully, both in securing a place to work and then in supplying them with food or they were exploited by unscrupulous employment agencies. Hull House made an investigation both of the padrone and of the agencies in our immediate vicinity, and the outcome confirming what we already suspected, we eagerly threw ourselves into a movement to procure free employment bureaus under State control until a law authorizing such bureaus and giving the officials entrusted with their management power to regulate private employment agencies passed the Illinois Legislature in 1899.

She noted that 10 years later, an investigation made by the League for the Protection of Immigrants revealed that aliens were still shamelessly imposed upon. She related how Hull House operated on behalf of its neighbors:

> The Superintendent of this League, Miss Grace Abbott, is a resident of Hull House, and all of our later attempts to obtain justice and opportunity for immigrants are much more effective, through the League, and when we speak before a congressional committee in Washington concerning the needs of Chicago immigrants, we represent the League as well as our own neighbors.

When the National Origins Act of 1924 established quotas for each country outside the Western Hemisphere, she pointed out its injustice and the hardships it imposed, especially on eastern and southern Europeans and Japanese.

Jane recognized that there would always be problems for most of the poor newcomers. The proportion of blacks to Europeans in Chicago had increased 20 years after the founding of Hull House when she wrote: "Perhaps no one so wistfully feels the need of a champion—certainly no one can need one more—than the negro."

Because of her rural roots, Jane had little familiarity with labor problems when she first settled in Chicago. However, she soon became sympathetic to the plight of the worker and considered the aims of trade unionism "immediately useful and practically attainable." The Women Shirt Makers, Women Cloak Makers, Dorcas Federal Labor Union, and Chicago Women's Trade Union League were all organized at Hull House. Jane believed in collective bargaining and during several strikes spoke out publicly on behalf of the strikers. She also hired union workers and used union-made products.

With regard to her role in two specific strikes, she said: "In the public excitement following the Pullman strike [1894] Hull-House lost many friends; later the teamsters' strike [1905] caused another such defection, although my office in both cases had been solely that of a duly appointed arbitrator." Although she was dependent upon continuing financial support from private sources, she could not let that interfere when she believed an unpopular position should be taken. She once turned down an offer of $20,000 for a new building because the donor "was notorious for underpaying the girls in his establishment and concerning whom there were even darker stories." Her independence is demonstrated by the following incident: During a discussion, she was once confronted with the accusation that "when you are subsidized by the millionaires, you will be afraid to talk like this." Jane replied that while she did not intend to be subsidized by millionaires, neither did she propose to be bullied by workingmen and that she would state her honest opinion without consulting either of them.

In sum, Jane's position on labor appears to have been moderate. As a member of the Chicago Board of Education (1905–1908), she disappointed the teachers by compromising in a dispute over promotions. Because she did not see an issue in black and white, she had the ability to make reasonable concessions. A pragmatist, she sometimes compromised.

She believed in persuasion through education. An accomplished speaker and writer, she authored 11 nonfiction books, including one that dealt with prostitution. She also wrote numerous articles on a variety of subjects—settlement life, industrial conditions, juvenile justice, woman suffrage, civil rights, municipal reform and planning, immigration and ethnicity, child welfare, international peace, and more. These articles appeared in professional journals and in some popular magazines.

Jane's liberal views brought her to the forefront in many causes. In 1909, she helped to found the National Association for the Advancement of Colored People. In 1913, she attended the Conference and Congress of International Woman's Suffrage in Budapest. In 1920, she was an organizer of the American Civil Liberties Union. Although she was in favor of votes for women, she did not support the Equal Rights Amendment. This was because she had fought for protective legislation for women workers and did not want to change her stance on this.

In common with most settlement workers of the 1920s, she supported the Volsted Act (Prohibition). After discussing the crime and resistance associated with it, she made it clear in 1930 that she wanted to see it survive. She made this analogy:

> During many years thousands of former slaves, legally freed by the Fourteenth Amendment to the Constitution, found themselves in the midst of a population who were theoretically and practically averse to their freedom. Some of the former slaves were scarcely more free than they had been before, some of them fell into a sort of peonage and many of them were gradually deprived of the franchise given to them for their own defense. And yet, could anyone say that this amendment was not to the great advantage of the citizens of the United States, nor deny that after two generations of even pseudo freedom the negroes have had an enormous advantage over their forebearers?

Jane's views on working mothers are not in accord with modern feminist thinking. She once referred to "that wretched delusion that a woman can both support and nurture her children." Such an utterance was perhaps colored by the fact that she was familiar with children who had suffered serious injuries when unattended at home while their mothers were at work, and in summer Hull House was often a refuge for little children who were left unsupervised in apartments or tenements that became uncomfortably hot.

Jane was a steadfast pacifist, refusing to be moved by World War I hysteria and criticism that she was unpatriotic. In 1915, she was elected first chairman of the Woman's Peace Party, which she helped to organize. She also presided at the International Congress for Women at the Hague, appealing for women to unite to stop the fighting. She later stated her sentiments: "Whenever war is declared ... patriotism is reduced to the basic appeal of self-defense. Thousands of men marched to their death because they have been convinced that they must serve their country. It is one of the finest instincts of the human spirit but is unworthy of modern civilization to utilize it at so fearful a cost." In 1919, she founded the Women's International League for Peace and Freedom and served as its president until 1929. By this time, she had become a firm advocate of internationalism. In 1931, she became the first American woman recipient of the Nobel Peace Prize, which honor she shared with educator Nicholas Murray Butler.

Jane Addams died in 1935. She had received numerous honors and had at one time been the best-known and most respected woman in the

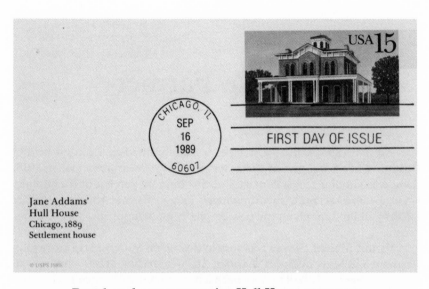

Jane Addams'
Hull House
Chicago, 1889
Settlement house

Postal card commemorating Hull House centenary.

United States. One of the most poignant tributes to her appeared in a Greek newspaper. It was written by a columnist, a man who had frequented Hull House in his youth: "We of foreign birth have lost our best friend and the only one who understood us." A Jane Addams 10-cent postage stamp was issued in 1940.

During the 1960s, the University of Illinois at Chicago took over Hull House Association's holdings to make room for a new campus. Today all that remains of the 13-building complex are the original Hull mansion and the residents' dining hall. Both have been restored and opened to the public. In 1967, Hull House was designated as a National Historic Landmark.

Hull House Association continues to serve metropolitan Chicago from new headquarters. The racial and ethnic mix of the people served has changed; there are more senior citizens than in Jane's day; the drug problem is serious; there is more crime. But in the spirit of Jane Addams, the large number of community centers that are part of the association strive to meet the problems of their neighbors.

Fannie Farmer

Around 1895, some 800 recipes were submitted to a contest held in Boston. Only 5 percent of them specified level measurements. In 1913, there was another recipe contest, but this time 90 percent of the submissions specified accurate measurements. Fannie Farmer believed that her efforts had brought about the new emphasis on definite amounts of ingredients.

Fannie Merritt Farmer was born in Boston on March 23, 1857, to John Franklin and Mary (Watson) Farmer. She was the first of four children, all girls. Mr. Farmer is said to have been a newspaperman turned printer, but there is some question about this. At any rate, he provided a comfortable middle-class home for his family. The Farmers moved to Medford, close to Boston, when Fannie was a child. There she attended Medford High School and the Unitarian Church. At 17 she suffered some sort of a paralytic illness. There is speculation whether she had poliomyelitis or a cerebral hemorrhage. Whatever happened, she was left with a permanent limp. As the years passed, Mr. Farmer suffered financial losses, reportedly largely because he held to a hand press rather than modernizing. To help out, Fannie tried her hand "in trade" (clerking) and later as a "mother's helper" (domestic work) at the home of a family friend, a Mrs. Charles Shaw.

Under Mrs. Shaw, Fannie gained confidence in cooking. Encouraged by her family and Shaw, she enrolled in 1887 at the Boston Cooking School, which had been established 10 years earlier by the Women's Education Association. The school's mission was to train cooking teachers for public and private schools and to train women to be professional cooks. Presumably, Fannie was seeking a means of earning a living in a field that was beginning to hold her interest. She did well in the two-year course, which included theory. The year following graduation saw her employed as assistant to the school's director, Carrie Dearborn. Following Dearborn's death, Fannie was appointed to the position in 1891. This enabled her to give her family financial assistance.

In 1896, Little Brown printed 3,000 copies of Fanny's *The Boston Cooking-School Cook Book*. The publisher appears to have had little con-

Fannie Merritt Farmer (date unknown). Courtesy of the Boston Public Library, Print Department. Fannie did not permit her publisher to use her portrait in *The Boston Cooking-School Cook Book.*

fidence in the venture, for it was done at the author's expense. In an article for the *Woman's Home Companion* in December 1915, Mary Bronson Hartt explained the rationale of a cooking-school cookbook:

> A cooking-school cook book is infinitely superior to a one-woman cook book because it represents the experimental wisdom of many. The

average cook book is a compilation from miscellaneous sources. Not a tithe of the recipes, perhaps, have been actually tested by the author. The expense of materials and the time necessary for such wholesale testing would more than eat up the profits of the book.

But in a cooking-school each recipe can be tested, not by one individual but by whole classes. If the directions are faulty, somebody is sure to discover the weak spot. Ingenious pupils frequently suggest improvements of the original recipe, and the faculty can always be set to experimenting upon a recipe which seems to fall just short of perfection.

Miss Farmer, by the title, was claiming for her book not only her own immensely careful and scientific experimenting, but the critical judgment of faculty and pupils during a period of eleven years.

The book became a great success, and we shall have more to say about that later.

In 1902, Fannie resigned her position at the Boston Cooking School and started her own establishment, Miss Farmer's School of Cookery, employing five assistant teachers and five maids. She was now able to give a more individualized type of instruction, teaching housewives, society girls, professional cooks, and those responsible for the nutrition and feeding of the sick. According to her niece-in-law, "Aunt Fannie was a great executive, food detective, and gourmet rather than a great cook herself." Others have rated her an excellent cook, but it has been noted that at her lectures someone else usually did the actual cooking because Fannie was "too impatient."

Although Fannie was regarded as shy and reserved, she was popular as a lecturer. Noted for wearing a pince-nez, she was red-haired, plump, and rather plain. However, her vivacious personality seemed to overshadow her appearance. In contrast to the small classes of eight so often offered at the school, her weekly demonstration lectures sometimes brought audiences of 150 to 200. The *Boston Transcript* regularly reported these talks, and they were reprinted elsewhere. Fannie was often sought to speak to women's clubs and similar groups. She once went on a lecture tour that took her to various parts of the country.

With the help of her sister, Cora Dexter Perkins, Fannie wrote a popular page on cooking for the monthly magazine, the *Woman's Home Companion*. She began this in 1905 and faithfully continued it until 1915. Her pieces included "Cooking the Cheaper Meats" and "Twenty Good Sandwiches."

She wrote other books besides *The Boston Cooking-School Cook Book: Chafing Dish Possibilities* (1898), *What to Have for Dinner* (1905), *Catering for Special Occasions with Menus and Recipes* (1911), and *A New Book of Cookery* (1912). It is said that she was especially proud of *Food and Cookery for the Sick and Convalescent,* published in 1904.

Professional dieticians as we know them today were yet to come. The

1904 advertisement for Fannie Farmer's books.

preface of the 1904 book mentions "the numberless classes of trained nurses whom it has been my pleasure and privilege to instruct during my thirteen years of service as a teacher of cookery." Not only was she involved in teaching Invalid Cookery in hospitals; she also conducted one course for students (all male) at Harvard Medical School. The same preface stated:

> Emphasis has been laid on the importance of diet from infancy to old age. The classification, composition, nutritive value, and digestibility of foods have been carefully considered with the same constant purpose of being a help to those who arrange dietaries. The chapter on infant feeding is an authoritative guide to aid in the development of the baby, while child feeding is considered with like care. Considerable matter has been introduced with reference to diet in various diseases.

At the time this was written, knowledge about nutrition was increasing rapidly. It was not known, however, why sufficient food alone might fail to sustain life. In 1906, British biochemist Gowland Hopkins concluded from his experiments that there were "indispensable ingredients in the food." Six years later, Casimir Funk, the Polish-American biochemist, proposed the name "vitamine" for such substances. (He assumed that the necessary ingredients belonged to a group of chemicals known as amines; to this he added *vita,* the Latin word for "life." Now it is known that vitamins are represented by other chemical groups besides amines.) So *Food and Cookery for the Sick and Convalescent* was too early to provide practical prevention, based on theory, of certain deficiency diseases of children and adults. The isolation and determination of the chemical structure of individual vitamins continued well into this century.

Here is an excerpt from the chapter on diabetes mellitus:

> Diabetes is essentially a dietetic disease. No drug or medicinal remedy has yet been found which is curative, but prescribed diet keeps the disease under control, and unless the case is severe and of long standing sugar may entirely disappear from the urine. It might seem from this statement that diabetic cures have been accomplished, though such is the case only with the rarest exception. If the patient returned to his ordinary mixed diet, sugar would reappear in the urine.
>
> When the disease develops in childhood, but little can be done to help the sufferer, and the patient lives but a few weeks, or at best a few months.... When the disease develops in adults, life may be prolonged and made pleasurable for many years, and death often follows from other causes than diabetes.

Here again we see a reflection of the knowledge of the day: for the treatment of insulin-dependent diabetes, that hormone did not become readily available until the 1920s, thanks to the work of Canadian physician

Frederick Banting and its commercial development by Eli Lilly and Company of Indianapolis.

Nevertheless, Fannie's writing shows that she was well informed with regard to what today is called "state of the art." For example, the book's references to sterilization and pasteurization show that she understood the germ theory of disease; in fact, she lived through the period known as bacteriology's "golden age."

During the last seven years of her life, Fannie's legs were paralyzed. Nevertheless, with courage and spirit, she lectured from a wheelchair. Despite advancing renal disease, which she knew spelled her doom, she continued to work. She delivered her last lecture 10 days before she died in 1915.

The family continued to revise *The Boston Cooking-School* book, holding the copyright until 1965. At that time, Dexter Perkins, Fannie's adored nephew, and his wife, Wilma Lord Perkins, sold the rights to Fanny Farmer Candy Shops, Inc. Mrs. Perkins had served continuously as editor from 1930. By 1974, the work had gone through 11 revised editions and sold almost 4 million copies. Of course, it was necessary that continuous changes be made to meet the conditions of the day. After the tenth edition, the title became *The Fannie Farmer Cookbook*. The Fanny Farmer Candy Shops selected Alfred Knopf as publisher. A facsimile of the 1896 edition remains in print, as does a large-print issue of the twelfth edition. *The Boston Cooking-School Cook Book* was translated into several languages, and a Braille edition was made.

The school continued until 1944. Alice Bradley, an instructor at Miss Farmer's School of Cookery, became principal and owner.

What made this book such an outstanding success? Here is one clue: Writing in *The American Heritage Cookbook,* Russell Lynes quotes Lillian W. Betts, who complained in 1895 that cookbooks were "not scientific." According to her, "The housekeeper must now fit herself to separate the chaff from the wheat when reading them, and if she is wise she will cull the best into a book of her own, after experiment and investigation."

Fannie's writings give indications that she had a scientific mind. Wilbur Atwater (1864–1907) and others had concerned themselves with caloric value—the amount of energy supplied by food—and data of this sort, along with a brief explanation of how the body utilizes various foodstuffs, appeared in Fannie's most famous cookbook. In its preface, as in the one for the sick, she emphasized the role of diet, this time in health: "I certainly feel that the time is not too far distant when a knowledge of the principles of diet will be an essential part of one's education. . . . It is my wish that [this book] may awaken an interest through its condensed scientific knowledge which will lead to deeper thought and broader study of what to eat."

Perhaps it was this scientific bent that spurred her crusade for exact measurement in cookery. "Correct measurements are absolutely necessary to insure the best results," she wrote. Under "Measuring Ingredients" is this information:

> Flour, meal, powdered and confectioners' sugar, and soda should be sifted before measuring. Mustard and baking powder, from standing in boxes, settle, therefore should be stirred to lighten; salt frequently lumps, and these lumps should be broken. A *cupful* is measured level. To measure a cupful, put in the ingredient by spoonfuls or from a scoop, round slightly, and level with a case knife, care being taken not to shake the cup. . . .
> To measure tea or tablespoonfuls, dip the spoon in the ingredient, fill, lift, and level with a knife, the sharp edge of knife being toward tip of spoon. Divide with knife lengthwise of spoon, for a half spoonful; divide halves crosswise for quarters, and quarters crosswise for eighths. Less than one-eighth of a teaspoonful is considered a few grains.

In contrast to the above, *Beeton's Book of Household Management*—first published as a bound edition in 1861 and although British, considered one of the best authorities of its day—presented little to encourage careful measurement. To illustrate, a muffin recipe directed, "To every quart of milk, allow 1½ oz. of German yeast, a little salt; flour . . . stir in sufficient flour to make the whole into a dough of rather a soft consistence." Another Beeton recipe recommended "sugar to taste." And so it went in pre–*Boston Cooking-School* days. Fannie, with reason, is sometimes referred to as the "Mother of Level Measurement."

The field testing that Fannie's recipes underwent should have done much toward making unnecessary Betts's suggestion about the creation of individual cookbooks.

In contrast to the immigrants who were Jane Addams's concern, Fannie's intended market was the large number of middle-class families. Thus the recipes of *The Boston Cooking-School Cook Book* were designed for an average family of six with not more than one servant. This was practical, in light of the projection that in 1900 American women were bearing an average of 3.56 children.

In fact, *practical* was a key word to describe the book. "Various oven thermometers have been made," Fannie wrote, "but none have proved practical." For this reason, the book did not advocate their use, at least until better instruments became available.

There are many examples of thrift—among them suggestions for uses of stale bread, ways to use remnants of cooked fish, and ideas about warmed-over potatoes, beef, and the like. In discussing a cooking stove, she observed: "Ashes must be removed and sifted daily; pick over and save good coals—which are known as cinders—throwing out useless pieces, known as clinkers."

It is possible that Fannie's thrust for economy was influenced by a contemporary Bostonian, Ellen Swallow Richards. The first woman to be admitted to Massachusetts Institute of Technology, Richards in 1890 played a major role in setting up Boston's New England Kitchen to help solve "one of the greatest problems of the age—how the poor might be economically and well fed."

With regard to nondietary activities, Fannie's famous book has a short chapter, "Helpful Hints for the Young Housekeeper." Here one reads advice such as

To keep a **Sink Drain** free from grease, pour down once a week at night one-half can Babbitt's potash dissolved in one quart water.

Should **Sink Drain** chance to get choked, pour into sink one-fourth pound copperas dissolved in two quarts boiling water. If this is not efficacious, repeat before sending for a plumber.

To prevent **Glassware** from being easily broken, put in a kettle of cold water, heat gradually until water has reached boiling-point. Set aside; when water is cold take out glass. This is a most desirable way to toughen lamp chimneys.

A bottle containing **Oxalic Acid** should be marked poison and kept on a high shelf.

To keep an **Ice Chest** in good condition, wash thoroughly once a week with cold or lukewarm water in which washing soda has been dissolved. If by chance anything is spilt in an ice chest, it should be wiped off at once. Milk and butter very quickly absorb odors, and if in an ice chest with other foods, should be kept closely covered.

The recipes vary from simple to complicated:

Cheap Sponge Cake

Yolks 3 eggs	1½ teaspoons baking
1 cup sugar	powder
1 tablespoon hot water	¼ teaspoon salt
a cup flour	Whites 3 eggs
2 teaspoons vinegar	

Beat yolks of eggs until thick and lemon-colored, add sugar gradually, and continue beating; then add water, flour mixed and sifted with baking powder and salt, whites of egg beaten until stiff, and vinegar. Bake thirty-five minutes in a moderate oven, in a buttered and floured cake pan.

Wedding Cake II

1 lb. butter	3 lbs. raisins, seeded
1 lb. brown sugar	and cut in pieces
12 eggs	2 lbs. Sultana raisins
1 cup molasses	1½ lbs. citron, thinly
1 lb. flour	sliced and cut in
4 teaspoons cinnamon	strips

4 teaspoons allspice	1 lb. currants
1½ teaspoons mace	½ preserved lemon
1 nutmeg, grated	rind
¼ teaspoon soda	½ preserved orange
1 tablespoon hot water	rind
4 squares chocolate,	1 cup brandy
melted	

Cream the butter, add sugar gradually, and beat thoroughly. Separate yolks from whites of eggs, and beat yolks until thick and lemon colored. Add to first mixture, then add flour (excepting one third cup, which should be reserved to dredge fruit), mixed and sifted with spices, fruit dredged with flour, lemon rind and orange rind finely chopped, brandy, chocolate, and whites of eggs beaten until stiff and dry. Just before putting into pans, add soda dissolved in hot water. Cover pans with buttered paper, and steam four hours. Finish cooking by leaving in warm oven over night.

The recipe for Boston Baked Beans dispelled a myth of the day with this: "The fine reputation which Boston Baked Beans have gained has been attributed to the earthen bean-pot with small top and bulging sides, in which they are supposed to be cooked. Equally good beans have often been eaten where a five-pound lard pail was substituted for the broken bean-pot."

One recipe (of two) for brownies specified molasses, with no mention of chocolate.

The chapter "Suitable Combinations for Serving" suggested a mouth-watering **Menu for New England Thanksgiving Dinner:**

Oyster Soup   Crisp Crackers
Celery   Salted Almonds
Roast Stuffed Turkey Giblet Gravy Cranberry Jelly
Mashed Potatoes Onions in Cream Turnips
Chicken Pie
Thanksgiving Pudding   Stirling Sauce
Mince, Apple, and Squash Pie
Vanilla Ice Cream   Fancy Cakes
Fruit Nuts and Raisins Bonbons
Crackers Cheese Cafe Noir

The Fanny Farmer Candy Shops, Inc., owns all rights to the name Fannie Farmer. (The founder of the candy company, Frank O'Connor, was impressed with Fannie's story and named his business in her honor.) Between the cookbook and the candy, Fannie Farmer endures as a household word.

It has been said that Fannie Farmer, like her father, was slow to change old ways. Nevertheless, it is interesting to speculate about her productivity were she brought back to earth today. Perhaps she would reject microwave cooking. But is it not conceivable that we would soon be eating all sorts of low-calorie, low-fat delectables made according to Fannie's field-tested recipes?

Lillian D. Wald

Today nurses are taken for granted as part of the public-school system. Although diphtheria, measles, scarlet fever, and skin and eye conditions afflicted thousands of children attending schools at the turn of this century, the school nurse was unknown. That situation changed in 1902, thanks to the vision and efforts in New York City of Lillian Wald. The success of the school-nurse program was one of the early steps in the development and adoption of public-health nursing in the United States.

Lillian Wald was born on March 10, 1867, into an affluent and cultured Jewish family. Both her mother and father were immigrants, brought here as children from Germany and Poland, respectively. Her birthplace was Cincinnati, but the Walds were associated mainly with Rochester, New York, where Max Wald dealt in optical wares. Lillian's childhood was happy, and according to her, she had the advantage of a good education. She knew Latin and spoke French and German. (She did not speak Yiddish, and sometimes in pursuing her lifework was forced to rely on German.) By the age of 21, she felt "the need of definite work." She had no plans for marriage; in fact, she never married.

To fill the need she felt, she chose nursing, enrolling in the New York Hospital Training School for Nurses. Such schools were relatively new in the United States and their graduates few in number. She finished the two-year course in 1891 and took a position at the New York Juvenile Asylum.

The work there was not to Lillian's liking. Like Jane Addams, she tried medicine and was admitted to the Women's Medical College in New York. While a student there, she taught home nursing to immigrant families on the Lower East Side. Through this venture she found her true vocation.

The Lower East Side was occupied by immigrants—Jewish, for the most part, Irish, German, and Italian—who were packed into decaying, dank, airless, unsanitary dwellings whose landlords were interested only in profit. To pay their rent, most tenants were forced to take in roomers, thereby intensifying a bad situation. Disease was rampant and crime almost as serious a problem. The deplorable conditions of such tenement houses had been eloquently described in Jacob Riis's 1890 book, *How the Other Half Lives*. A 1903 report stated: "The most terrible of all the features of tenement house life in New York, however, is the indiscriminate herding of all kinds of people in close contact, the fact that, mingled with the drunken, the dissolute, the improvident, the diseased, dwell the great mass of the respectable workingmen of the city with their families."

One day a member of the class Lillian was instructing was absent. However, a small child appeared at the school on Henry Street where the class was in progress. She said her mother was sick. Lillian followed the child past unspeakable filth to her home and found a young woman who had delivered two days previously. Covered with dried blood, she lay in bed in squalor.

Although she was then a stranger to the problems of the poor, what she had seen that day convinced Lillian that she could be of service among the people of the Lower East Side. She quit her medical studies and began to pursue an idea that had come to her. As we shall see, her work more and more paralleled Jane Addams's. However, in the beginning, Lillian's primary focus was on providing home nursing to the people crowded into 20 city blocks that constituted the Lower East Side, people who lived in poverty, dependent on charity, not government, when added misfortune struck.

To convert her dream to action, Lillian approached Mrs. Solomon Loeb, the sponsor of the class the nurse–medical student had been teaching. Loeb found this young woman "either crazy or a genius," and agreed to help. The aid of the Loebs's son-in-law, financier Jacob Schiff, was also enlisted. They promised to donate $120 per month to cover supplies and living expenses for two nurses.

Mary Brewster, also a graduate of New York Hospital Training School for Nurses and a descendant of William Brewster of Plymouth-colony fame, was chosen as the second nurse to work with Lillian. The two women were "to live in the neighborhood as nurses, identify ourselves with it socially and . . . contribute to it our citizenship." Note the similarity of this sentiment to Jane Addams's when she and Ellen Starr moved into Hull House.

Their first residence was the new College Settlement on Rivington Street, where they remained briefly but long enough to learn about the settlement movement. In September 1893, they moved to the top floor of a tenement house located at Jefferson Street, one of the few places with a private bathtub. (Private toilets were very rare at the time.)

They were ready to help wherever needed, and it was not difficult to find patients. Hospitals were feared and avoided; the sick for the most part remained at home with little professional care. Mr. Schiff required written reports, which the nurses prepared meticulously. He was informed that they found children "scarred with vermin bites"; a young girl dying of tuberculosis; adults with typhoid fever; "a crazy woman . . . ill from typhoid and pneumonia, cared for by a father and fourteen-year-old daughter, who feared to tell lest she be taken to an asylum." And so it went.

Professional home nursing was almost nonexistent in this country. When offered, it was usually as a charity provided under religious auspices. Sensing that the East Siders despised charity, which was usually associated with organized religion, Lillian made nursing services available to anyone, regardless of religion or race. To avoid the stigma of charity, a charge of 10 cents per visit was made but not collected if it would impose hardship. Cases came to the nurses' attention by word of mouth and their literally knocking on doors.

Almost immediately it was clear that more nurses were needed, and Mr. Schiff agreed to finance one. From the beginning, the nurses made little separation between the medical and social needs of the families they encountered. These women soon learned to have their clients make use of offers of free ice, free clothing, free tickets to summer excursions, and the like. But the economic and social needs of their neighbors presented a continuing complex and time-consuming problem. Early in her career Lillian wrote to her mentor: "The burden of the family is felt in other ways than disease, for work must be procured some way, somehow, and indeed we are not forgetful that means of bringing other relief than healing have been placed in our hands."

Lillian was quick to recognize that education would be the keynote for success in her work. In those preantibiotic days, prevention of disease was extremely important. It was necessary to emphasize, for example, that tuberculosis could be spread by the sputum of a person with active disease, that fecal material from a typhoid patient was dangerous, and so on.

Insistence on cleanliness was very important, but keeping clean was difficult for people who lived under such marginal conditions. Lillian did not give up. One of her reports stated, "I went into every room in the front and rear tenements, set the dwellers to sweeping, cleaning and *burning* the refuse. In some rooms swill thrown on the floor, vessels standing in the room unemptied from the night's use."

Good nutrition was another problem. Few people had even an adequate diet. Many of the immigrants knew nothing about preparing American food. It is not surprising to find that early in this century Lillian was advocating "a regular system of school lunches, dignified and orderly, in conformity with the theory of state responsibility for the best development of the child."

Despite the inherent difficulties, the nurses attacked problems to the best of their abilities. Some of Lillian's reports to Mr. Schiff reflect their activities.

Brought clean dresses to the older children and gave *Herald* ice ticket. I asked the editor of the *Herald* to substitute bread for ice because . . . there was nothing to put on the ice.

Samuel Shalinke's wife very ill, whom we nursed but finally induced to go to the hospital, where she died, her baby was then placed at Infant's Hospital . . . and for Samuel himself, work was found by Miss Brewster's people in Pennsylvania.

Jacob Schiff persuaded the New York Health Department to give approval to the nurses' work. Soon they were wearing badges inscribed *Visiting Nurses Under the Auspices of the Board of Health.* Lillian continued to maintain strong ties with this board. When Hermann Biggs, the distinguished commissioner of public health, called for reporting of cases of tuberculosis, he found that the Henry Street group had been keeping a list of such patients. In time, the care provided by Lillian's nurses impressed the Board of Health; for example, in 1917, New York City appropriated $25,000 to the service. Although public-health nursing as such was still unknown, Lillian Wald was practicing many of its underlying principles.

By April 1895, the Visiting Nurses Service had a new base located at 265 Henry Street beside the Louis Technical School where Lillian had conducted classes when she was a medical student. The benefactor was the generous Schiff, who also paid for needed repairs. So was born the Henry Street Settlement where Lillian Wald resided and worked for the next 40 years. (Mary Brewster soon had to leave because of poor health.)

More nurses were recruited. They lived in the settlement house and worked in the neighborhood. Among them was Lavinia Dock, a Bellevue Hospital graduate with experience in nursing and nursing education. She was also a fiery suffragist and a pacifist. She became a fast friend of Lillian, giving her valuable professional advice. By 1900, there were 15 residents. Philanthropy, not municipal funds, was the mainstay of the project, and Lillian was the prime mover in obtaining funds from the wealthy. Fortunately she had charm, was persuasive, and had the ability to impress people with her sincerity and clear purpose. Grants from such people as Henry Morgenthau and groups such as the directors of Presbyterian Hospital often paid individual salaries. In a 1907 speech, "Best Helps to the Immigrant through the Nurse," she said:

District nursing of today follows the tradition of its earliest conception. It has been used since the beginning of its history to carry propaganda as there has been always an enthusiastic belief in the possibility of the nurse as teacher in religion, cleanliness, temperance, cooking, housekeeping, etc. My argument loses none of its force, I think, if much of this education has seemed to her lost energy because with greater knowledge and wider experience she has learned that the individual is not so often to blame, as she at first supposed. That while the district nurse is laboring with the individual she should also contribute her knowledge towards the study of the large general conditions of which her poor patient may be the victim.

Many of these conditions seem hopelessly bad but many are capable of prevention and cure when the public shall be stimulated to a realization of the wrong to the individual as well as to society in general if [they] are permitted to persist. Therefore her knowledge of the laws that have been enacted to prevent and cure, and her intelligence in recording and reporting the general as well as the individual conditions that make for degradation and social iniquity are but an advance from her readiness to instruct and correct personal and family hygiene to giving attention to home sanitation and then to city sanitation, an advance from the individual to the collective interest. The subject is tremendously important, even exciting, and adds the glamor of a wide patriotic significance to the daily hard work of the nurse. The prevalence of tuberculosis, for instance, brings attention directly to conditions of industry and housing, next to hours of work, to legal restrictions, to indifference to the laws, to possible abuse of the weaker for the benefit of the stronger.

It is splendid vindication of the value of comprehensive education and stimulated social conscience that the district nurses who have had this vision have been the most faithful and hard working and zealous in their actual care of the sick.... [The] wider vision [of the district nurse] makes for thoroughness as an all important educational, social and humanitarian necessity where the patients are concerned.

These opportunities ... bear the closest relationship to the immigrants, because they are the most helpless of our population and the most exploited; the least informed and instructed in the very matters that are essential to their happiness. The country needs them and uses them and it is obviously an obligation due them as well as safe guarding of the country itself to give them intelligent conception and education of what is important to their and to our interests.

During a trip abroad, Lillian learned that a British philanthropist had provided for a nurse in one of the London schools. In New York, Lillian's suggestion for such a school nurse fell on deaf ears at first. There was some progress in supplying doctors, but the service was quite inadequate. Meanwhile, pupils with various contagious diseases often remained in school, and there was little follow-up on those who might be recovered sufficiently to return to school. After two years, the health commissioner requested assistance. Lillian selected Lina Rogers, a Henry Street nurse, to work on an experiment aimed at identifying, treating, and educating about conditions common in the school population. The demonstration proved to be so successful that before long 12 full-time nurses were hired to work in the schools. Officials saw the advantages of employing a school nurse, and soon the idea gained wide acceptance in the nation.

Convinced that rural areas would benefit from public-health nursing, in 1908 Lillian persuaded Mr. Schiff to give a grant of $100,000 to the American Red Cross to establish a Department of Town and Country Nursing.

Around this time, Henry House became involved with the Metropolitan Life Insurance Company in a unique venture. "Industrial insurance," first developed in England, had been adopted by Metropolitan. Sold door to door to poor city industrial workers, mostly immigrants, by agents who also collected a weekly premium of 3 to 10 cents, a medical examination was not required, and women and children were accepted. This scheme had the backing of the company's vice president, Haley Fiske, who regarded it as means of teaching the immigrants American values.

Fiske hired Lee Frankel as manager of his company's newly created Welfare Division. Frankel had worked extensively to improve conditions for Jewish immigrant workers. With 20 percent of Metropolitan's death claims due to tuberculosis, he planned to attack disease among the policyholders, beginning with that scourge. He intended to write a leaflet about TB and have it distributed by the agents.

When Lillian heard Frankel describe his plan, she suggested that nurses could be more effective than his agents as teachers of health education. Statistics from Henry Street convinced Metropolitan's Board of Directors that nursing visits reduced mortality rates, and a plan for a three-month pilot project was drawn up. Agents would provide visiting nurses with a list of the industrial policyholders who had requested medical assistance. The insurance company agreed to pay 50 cents per visit for the provision of health care and health education to its policyholders in New York's Tribeca area. There would be no charge to the policyholder.

Nurse Ada Bagley reported to Metropolitan's Broadway office on June 9, 1909, for instructions. Her first patient, the first patient to receive service under the new cooperative plan, was Ellen Daly, an Irish immigrant who had leg ulcers as a result of varicosities and was also suffering from isolation.

The pilot project went so well that it was instituted for Metropolitan policyholders throughout Manhattan and extended to other cities. This service continued until 1953. Besides providing home care to millions, it produced Metropolitan's famous pamphlets on tuberculosis, whooping cough, and so on. The latter were supplied to policyholders by agents and nurses.

Because she recognized the growing need for nursing instructors, Lillian convinced yet another philanthropist, Helen Hartley Jenkins, that Columbia University Teachers College would be a worthy recipient of money for that purpose. Over the years, Lillian encouraged close ties between Henry Street and Teachers College.

Ten years after its establishment, the Henry Street Visiting Nurses Service had headquarters consisting of seven buildings on Henry Street (including the Louis Technical School), branches in Upper Manhattan and the Bronx, and a small facility for convalescents. A staff of 92 nurses now

offered home care and maintained first-aid stations as well as centers that distributed uncontaminated milk. Incidentally, Margaret Sanger, whom we shall meet later, was associated with Henry Street Settlement in 1912.

During the influenza epidemic of 1918, the visiting nurses did yeoman service. This highly infectious viral disease was often accompanied by a virulent and fatal pneumonia. (Before the pandemic subsided, it took the lives of 2 million.) On October 10, under the Red Cross, New York City's Nurses' Emergency Council was formed, with Lillian as its head. The situation was grim. "War needs had depleted available hospital beds, doctors, nurses, druggists and supplies," she reported later. (There were even too few laundresses, graves, gravediggers, and shroud makers.) Drawing on her experience and using her organizational ability, Lillian pressed into service every agency she knew. Volunteers from all walks of life were recruited. According to her, "Business men, bankers and members of the Salvation Army went side by side into the hospitals to serve as orderlies.... College girls and society women assisted with the hospital dishwashing." Her nurses were put on 24-hour duty, working in 8-hour shifts. The need was great since often every member of the family was stricken, helpless to do anything. Later Lillian received kudos from the city and its Board of Health. She used the experience of the epidemic to emphasize that "more trained nurses are needed in the communities, not only to care for the sick, but also to teach while they are giving nursing care."

The Visiting Nurses Service did continue to grow. Mr. Schiff died in 1920, leaving it $300,000 for a central administration building on Park Avenue. Eventually the nursing service was separated from the settlement. In 1944 it became the Visiting Nurse Service of New York. Lillian was dead then, but surely she would have been proud to see the expansion of a service that had begun some 50 years before with the activities of two competent and dedicated young nurses.

In keeping with the severance of the nursing program, Lillian's immediate successor as director of Henry House settlement was Helen Hall, whose training was in social work. In a 1971 book, *Unfinished Business,* Hall described her 34 years at the settlement—years that saw the Depression, gang wars, drug addiction, and violence. With new generations from different parts of the world, never-ending problems, but problems all too familiar to Lillian, came to the fore: lack of decent housing, inadequate health care, low steady employment, and meager educational opportunities.

As with Hull House, the Henry Street Settlement instituted many

Opposite: **Visiting Nurse Service 1909. Lillian Wald is second from left in the front row. Courtesy of Metropolitan Life Insurance Company.**

activities aimed at bettering the life of the neighborhood's residents. Often there was no direct relationship to nursing. Now well aware of the existence of the people living around her, Lillian believed in winning the children "away from the limitations of their harsh and narrow world ... and into poetry and culture outside of their rough environment." The first non-nurse resident was Helen McDowell, who provided musical and theatrical programs attractive to children.

In 1895, the American Hero Club for boys came into existence. As its leader, Lillian provided inspiration by dramatizing historical figures who had attained success despite hardship. Over the years, numerous such clubs were formed, for girls as well as boys, even for mothers. The leader had talent or expertise in some area—music, carpentry, dance, and so on—and was given flexibility in organizing his or her unique program. The idea attracted various uptown people who found satisfaction in making life a little less drab for people less fortunate than themselves. One of the early leaders was Herbert Lehman, a future governor of New York and a liberal U.S. senator (in 1948, he and his wife gave a building to the Henry Street complex in memory of a son lost in World War II).

In keeping with her desire to expose the community to art, Lillian was an essential part of a campaign that successfully persuaded the Metropolitan Museum of Art to open on Sundays so that working people could enjoy its treasures. She understood the importance of recreation in the lives of her neighbors and played a role in getting New York City to provide parks and playgrounds for the deprived children of the area.

The diverse activities of the settlement attracted the attention of prominent and progressive people. Most visited and lent substantial support. By 1906, Henry Street Settlement had its first male resident.

From the beginning, plays and pageants were part of Henry Street Settlement. Two sisters, Alice and Irene Lewisohn, began to focus their talents on theatrical productions in 1907. In 1915, they deeded their Neighborhood Playhouse on Grand Street to the settlement. Supported by the Lewisohns, the playhouse presented experimental theater, giving young people an opportunity to train for the stage. This training encompassed costume making and set construction. Eventually the playhouse attracted professional actors and actresses and uptown audiences, but it kept contacts with the East Side. It presented musical programs, children's operettas, ballets, and ethnic plays.

Because of her close contact with the poor, Lillian Wald soon became a social activist—and a surprisingly successful one. In 1894, a Tenement House Committee headed by editor Richard Watson Gilder had made a classic report. Although Lillian had been suggested as a member of the committee, she had not been asked to serve on it. She deplored living conditions of the Lower East Side. The following is from a speech she made about crowded city districts:

> Read each figure [in the report] a human being; read that every wretched unlighted tenement described is a description of *homes* for people—men and women, young and old, with the strengths and weaknesses, the good and the bad, the appetites and wants that are common to all. Read in descriptions of sweatshops, factories and long-hour working days the difficulty, the impossibility of well-ordered living under them. Understanding reading of these things must bring a sense of fairness outraged, the disquieting conviction that something is wrong, and turning to your own contrast, you must feel a responsibility.

A few years after coming to Henry Street, Lillian met Elizabeth Farrell, a teacher at one of the neighborhood schools. Farrell was concerned about pupils who were unable to keep up academically with their classmates. Lillian supported this teacher's ideas on how to instruct such children. The upshot of this was that the Board of Education permitted the establishment of ungraded classes in the New York public schools. By 1915, 3,000 children were enrolled in what today would be termed special education.

As we have seen, Florence Kelley left Hull House in 1899 to become a resident at the Henry Street Settlement. At that time her position was general secretary of the new National Consumers League. Both she and Lillian worked hard and continuously to abolish child labor. By 1903, the state of New York had passed its first significant anti–child-labor law, but reforms were still needed.

In 1905, these two women conceived the idea of a federal Children's Bureau. "[It] would be a clearing house, a source of information, a reliable education, on all matters pertaining to the welfare of children and child life." Reliable data about children were lacking at the time. Lillian realized the value of such figures. According to her, the greatest aid in the reduction of the infant death rate would be "the full and current vital statistics of children, such as no one community can obtain for itself." (Today statistics are one of the keystones of public health.)

She presented her plan to a sympathetic Teddy Roosevelt, but seven years passed before the Children's Bureau came into existence. Its charge was to investigate and report on the affairs of children "among all classes of our people." The bureau soon concerned itself with prenatal health, which is intertwined with infant health. In deep despair when this country declared war on Germany on April 6, 1917, Lillian was heartened by the Children's Bureau's "Save the Baby Program," launched the same day and to be in effect for one year. (In New York City it provided medical examinations for all children younger than 5, ultimately revealing some sort of disorder in one out of three.) Today the bureau is part of the Department of Health and Human Services.

From her neighbors, Lillian learned something of the working conditions they endured—long hours (no 40-hour week at this time), poor pay, and poor working conditions that endangered health. She was especially sympathetic to women workers because of the low wages they were paid and sexual harassment. Recognizing that most unions did little or nothing for women, who generally did not remain for long as part of the work force, some forward-looking members of that sex formed the Women's Trade Union League, with Lillian a member of its executive board. The League demanded equal pay for equal work, an eight-hour day, and votes for women. Later they organized consumer boycotts and worked for issues such as fair-housing practices. In 1919, Lillian publicly supported union membership and collective bargaining.

Throughout her career, Lillian remained sympathetic to the viewpoint of the workingman. There was conflict here, however, for the success of her lifework was dependent on the capitalistic system through the largesse of successful people such as Jacob Schiff.

Although an advocate of many causes, Lillian seems to have considered peace the most important. A few weeks after war broke out in Europe in 1914, she joined 1,200 women of all ages and nationalities in a peace parade along Fifth Avenue. Before the march, she had declared, "Vital and fraternal relationships exist in this city between representatives of those nations who at this moment are intent upon mutual destruction." Later she expressed her opposition to giving help to the Allies: "I think we acknowledge that when we send relief, surgeons or nurses, the best that we have, to the field of battle, we are to some extent perpetuating and in a way glorifying war and its barbarisms. The countries that voluntarily go to war and spend huge sums for armaments and destructive weapons should face all the costs of war." In 1915, a group representing "conservative Quakers, socialism, the church, the press, literature and social work" formed the American Union against Militarism and made Lillian its president. As the United States became more involved in war preparations, there was a tendency to consider all pacifists pro–German. When testifying before the Senate Committee on Military Affairs, Lillian pointed out that "our nation has been infiltrated with militaristic propaganda." With the nation actually at war, the Union was weakened because of diverse beliefs among its members. Lillian resigned in September 1917 (the Union became a forerunner of today's American Civil Liberties Union).

Lillian had held that the United States "should not coerce men's conscience in a war of freedom." Consistent with this, she continued her public support of conscientious objectors, and Henry Street Settlement honored Jeanette Rankin, the Montana congresswoman who had voted against the

Lillian Wald, by Arnold Genthe (no date). Courtesy of the Library of Congress.

United States's declaration of war. In contrast, Lillian made available one of the settlement's buildings for the use of the draft board. The provision of nursing service was her chief concern, and wartime imposed great difficulties. For one thing, Anne Goodrich, her director of nurses, left temporarily to become dean of the Army School of Nursing. But Lillian Wald managed, looking forward to what could be done when peace came.

When it did come, she found herself with Jane Addams on the Military Intelligence Bureau's list of 62 people who, according to the *New York Times,* "had been recorded as active in movements which did not help the

United States when the country was fighting the Central Powers." As the "Red Scare" that followed the Russian Revolution swept this country, New York State empowered a committee to investigate radicalism in settlement houses and schools. Commenting on the committee's report, the *New York Telegram* in 1921 stated that the same two women were "anxious to bring about the overthrow of the government and establish in this country a soviet government on the same lines as Russia." Lillian's actions were successfully defended by the United Neighborhood Houses, but the publicity may have been detrimental to her cause.

Lillian's postwar years were filled with travel and conferences, international and national. The year 1919 was notable for one trip abroad; she represented the Children's Bureau at an International Red Cross Conference in France. Journeying on to Switzerland, she attended the International Conference of Women for Peace. Returning to France, she became an advisor to the League of Nations Child Welfare Division.

After stepping down as the head of Henry Street Settlement, Lillian lived at her home in Westport, Connecticut. By this time she had met many of the world's great and near-great—Jacob Riis, Sylvia Pankhurst, Lincoln Steffens, Eleanor and Franklin Roosevelt, Ida Tarbell, Willa Cather, Herbert Hoover, Ramsey MacDonald, John Galsworthy, and Albert Einstein, to name just a few. *The House on Henry Street* is Lillian's anecdotal autobiography, published in 1915. Its sequel appeared in 1934—*Windows on Henry House*. She died in 1940.

Lillian Wald was a leader endowed with skill in finding practical ways to solve problems. She was also a woman of vision; many of her ideas are in operation today. One of her primary concerns, the welfare of children, is met to some extent by government programs such as the WIC nutrition project, Headstart, Children's Special Health Care Services, Child Abuse and Neglect, Aid for Dependent Children, and so on. The efforts of the Department of Housing and Urban Development have had some success. At least there is now an awareness of the importance of decent housing for the poor—something long emphasized by Lillian. She would approve of the achievements of the unions in gaining fair wages, better hours, improved conditions in the workplace, and fringe benefits—most of which Lillian had urged.

Her views on religion and race were enlightened. Although Jewish, she respected individuals of all creeds. She once wrote: "Protestants, Catholics, Jews, an occasional Buddhist and those who claim no creed have lived and served together in the Henry House contented and happy, with no attempt to impose their theological convictions upon one another." In 1925, 4 million Americans belonged to the Ku Klux Klan, a bastion of racism and intolerance, and race relations were far worse than they are today. Yet in that same year, 20 percent of Lillian's staff were black. We should emphasize that strong as her convictions were on various issues, Lillian was no zealot.

Many honors came her way while she still lived. In 1970, she was elected to the Hall of Fame for Great Americans. Her enduring monument is related to nursing. *A History of Public Health,* authored by the distinguished authority George Rosen, lists Lillian Wald under "Memorable Figures in the History of Public Health" and states that she established public-health nursing in the United States.

Mary McLeod Bethune

This is the story of a determined and talented black woman. In contrast to Jane Addams, Fannie Farmer, and Lillian Wald, all of whom came from substantial backgrounds, Mary Bethune had little in the way of material goods. But we shall see that this did not deter her from her chosen course.

Mary, or Mary Jane as she was sometimes called, was born on July 10, 1875, near Mayesville, South Carolina, to Samuel and Patsy McLeod. Samuel and Patsy had been slaves on neighboring plantations. Samuel wanted to marry Patsy, so he had been hired out by his master to earn enough to buy her. Samuel was known as McLeod's Sam, and the couple took the master's name. They had 17 children, of whom Mary was the fifteenth. By the time she was born, emancipation had come, and later the family had been able to acquire several acres of their own on which the hardworking Samuel and his older sons had built a small cabin. They planted cotton on some of their acreage and raised rice where the land was swampy. Fish could be caught in a nearby stream; in the woods there were rabbits, opossum, and quail. In addition to all the demands involved in caring for so many children, Patsy worked in the fields and earned money doing laundry for whites. She also had a vegetable garden and had planted flowers, a fig tree, and a grape vine. A good manager with high principles, she was a fine role model for Mary.

The McLeods, thanks to their industry, had fared much better than many former slaves who remained sharecroppers (see page 114) through lack of opportunity or ambition. Nevertheless, while still a child, Mary noticed that the white children her age had a school to go to—a school barred to her because of the color of her skin. Gradually she became aware of the unfair treatment of the Negro in the post–Reconstruction South.

The Civil War had left great devastation in the region. Some relief was afforded by the federal Freedmen's Bureau, founded in 1865. With state officials loyal to the Republican administration in Washington, it furnished food, supplies, and medical services to refugees and former slaves; it established schools; it supervised contracts between freedmen and their employees; and it managed confiscated or abandoned lands, leasing and selling some to former slaves.

Expectation had run high. "Forty acres and a mule" was a popular slogan based on a rumor that the bureau was going to confiscate from white owners all their land except 200 acres per family and give the excess to Negroes in parcels of 40 acres. This never came about, although under the Southern Homestead Act of 1866 much public land was made available to settlers of any race.

Former slaves had great hope that their children would soon be educated. With aid from the bureau, some institutions such as Howard University, Hampton Institute, Atlanta University, and Fiske University were founded. In 1869, there were almost a thousand teachers in the freedmen's schools in the South. The majority of these were white women from the North, although some were white Southerners. The number of black teachers grew gradually. The Protestant churches were active in promoting the education of the Negro, and it was during this period that the black churches grew and became prominent, although religion had always played a major role in slave life.

The eminent historian John Hope Franklin contends that the Freedmen's Bureau, in spite of Southern hostility, performed a vastly important task before it ended in 1872. He points out that the greatest failure of Reconstruction was economic; at the end, both white and black workers in the South were suffering from want and privation.

Mary's wish to know how to read was fulfilled when the Presbyterian Board of Missions started a school for Negroes in Mayesville. Although every hand was needed for farmwork, Samuel and Patsy agreed to let Mary attend. It meant a five-mile walk to and from Mayesville, but that appeared to be of little concern to anyone.

The mission school—sometimes referred to as a teach-and-preach school—was primitive. At first it was held in one room of a shack in the Negro part of town. The next year, a new two-room building was constructed. For many years to come, this was the only school for blacks in Mayesville and the surrounding area. The children were fortunate in their teacher, Emma Wilson. Educated at Scotia Seminary in North Carolina, she had returned to the South to try to improve the lot of her race, and she hoped that some of her pupils would be inspired to continue her work when they received an education. The McLeod family was religious, and the preaching aspect of the school reinforced Mary's faith. She was particularly impressed that her teacher called herself *Miss* Wilson. White Southerners reserved Mr., Mrs., and Miss for themselves. When she was older, Mary insisted that white persons whom she did not know address her as Mrs. Bethune, not Mary.

By the time Mary was 12, she was ready for what we might consider high school. But where could she get such training? An opportunity came unexpectedly. The Mission Board had an offer from a white woman who

lived in Denver, Colorado. A Quaker, Mary Chrissman had saved enough to offer a scholarship to train a worthy black student to do the type of thing Wilson was engaged in. Wilson picked Mary and arranged for her to enter Scotia Seminary (later Barber-Scotia College) in Concord, North Carolina, a Presbyterian institution for black girls that emphasized religion and industrial education, Wilson's alma mater. Mary was overwhelmed with her good fortune. Later she said, "My earnest efforts for the hundreds of Negro girls in the Southland today are dedicated to the memory of this self-sacrificing woman who gave me my first real chance, and to the dear parents—father and mother—who cheerfully gave me up, leaving them lonely and sad, while I prepared for my life's work."

Scotia opened a new world to 12-year-old Mary. The 150-mile train ride from Mayesville to Concord was a first for her. To call home a building with more than one level was very different from living in the tiny McLeod cabin. It was a new experience to have only two people sleeping in a room—she and a girl from Greensboro, North Carolina. And she relished having a real bed of her own. There were some white teachers, and she was surprised to see blacks and whites eating together. Since the scholarship covered only part of her total expenses, Mary had to work her way doing ironing, cooking, cleaning, or whatever was required. In summer she found domestic work with various families.

During her seven years there, Mary obtained a high school education and completed something close to junior college. She enjoyed the academic courses, excelled in the voice training she received as a member of the choir, and became proficient in public speaking and debate. By the time graduation approached, she had decided that rather than help her people here in this country, she would go to "dark Africa" as "an earnest missionary."

Scotia's president had advised Mary that the desired training for an African ministry could be obtained at the Bible Institute for Home and Foreign Missions (now Moody Bible Institute) in Chicago. She was accepted in 1894, and again Chrissman helped with scholarship money. Thirty-six years later, Mary was able to meet Chrissman in person, then living in California.

In 1890, Anna Cooper, a Negro woman who taught Latin to students of her race in Washington, D.C., observed, "The majority of colored men do not yet think it is worthwhile that women aspire to higher education." Obviously, this attitude did not lessen Mary's intense determination to reach her goal (Caucasian men tended to hold the same opinion).

Opposite: **Mary McLeod (second row, center) with classmates at Moody Bible Institute (courtesy Moody Bible Institute archives, Chicago). Although the only black American enrolled, Mary had warm feelings for Moody.**

"There were no feelings of race at Moody," she once declared. "A love for the whole human family, regardless of creed, class or color entered my soul and remains with me, thank God, to this day." There was more opportunity to develop her singing, and people began to take notice of her beautiful contralto voice. The year's training completed, she asked the Presbyterian Board of Missions to place her in a station in Africa. She was crushed to find that there was nothing for her.

The board, however, had an opening in Augusta, Georgia, at Haines Normal and Industrial Institute, founded by a persevering and dynamic black woman named Lucy Laney. Beginning with almost no financial support, she had been able to attract substantial donations, and by 1895 had a mission school for more than 200 black children, many of whom boarded there. (In time, Mary sent her own son to Haines.) Mary threw her energy into Laney's project, also concerned about the large number of ragged and dirty children that inhabited the Negro section of the city and could not be accommodated at Haines. She soon organized them and provided religious instruction. With the help of faculty and students, she set up collections for clothes, soap, toothbrushes, and so on, to be delivered door to door with a message stressing cleanliness.

Back in the South again, Mary saw more clearly than ever the inequalities of opportunity for her race. Now an adult, she understand better the Negro's fear of lynching, the potential for violence, the uneasy state of race relations. (When women could vote, she deplored the poll tax, imposed to circumvent the right of the black to vote. Nevertheless, she urged her people to pay it to ensure their voice at the polls.)

Her next assignment was closer to home, in Sumter, South Carolina, at Kindell Institute, another mission school for blacks. She remained there for two years. During this time, she was helping two of her sisters through Scotia and was also sending every extra penny to her father. The family cabin had burned down, necessitating a new house, for which there was a mortgage on the farm. (Eventually she was able to provide a small comfortable home for her parents in Sumter, where they spent their last years cared for by their youngest daughter.)

In 1898, Mary married Albertus L. Bethune and moved to Savannah, Georgia, where he could earn a living. Their only child, Albert (Bert) McLeod Bethune, was born a year later. The marriage was not a success, and the couple parted after 10 years. Albertus appears to have had little interest in the altruistic ventures that became almost a compulsion with many. He died in 1919 of tuberculosis without achieving the financial success that he sought.

When the baby was less than a year old, Mary started a mission school in Palatka, Florida. She stayed for four years, not only building a successful school but extending the benefit of her missionary training to nearby lumber camps, turpentine stills, and the local jail. To add to her small salary, she sold policies for the Afro-American Life Insurance Company.

Inspired by the example of Lucy Laney's success with Haines, Mary began to dream of founding her own school for Negro girls. This idea developed into a crusade for her. In the previous century, Emma Willard had founded a school that provided higher education for women, realizing that this was a key to woman's advancement and independence. Mary Bethune saw clearly that education was a necessary and significant step in the Negro's rise to equal treatment. Toward the end of her life, she wrote something that gives us some insight into the thinking that prevailed as long as she lived:

> All my life I have worked with youth. I have begged for them and fought for them and lived for them and in them. Their story is my story.
>
> Because I see young Mary McLeod in all struggling boys and girls, I can never rest while there is still something that I can do to make the ground firmer under their feet, to make their efforts more productive, to bring their goals nearer, to make their faith in God and their fellow men a little stronger.

Obviously, she wanted her school where there was pressing need. Heeding the advice of a Baptist minister familiar with the situation, she traveled south 50 miles to look at Dayton, located on the Atlantic coast and the lagoonlike Halifax River. There the construction of the East Coast Railway had attracted many black day laborers, despite the fact that they were paid exploitive wages. The Negro section of the town was especially sordid — crowded and run-down. Mary knew that here there were children she could benefit. At the same time, she had her eye on the area inhabited by wealthy whites from all parts of the nation. Civic-minded men and women from winter and year-round homes could be approached for assistance. She had learned already that some women of this type had formed a group known as the Palmetto Club, noted for its philanthropy. She soon decided that Daytona was her spot (in 1926, Daytona and two other towns were incorporated as Daytona Beach).

She found a two-story frame building that rented for $11 a month. She did not have that amount in hand, but the owner let her have the place, trusting her to pay it later. Furnishing the building was not easy. She organized neighbors to scrounge for supplies and cast-off furniture, combing over dumps or anywhere else that might yield goods that could be repaired. She found boxes and packing cases that could be put to other uses; she went door to door begging not only for materials but money; she made sweet-potato pies and sold them to railroad workers.

By the end of a month, she was ready. On October 3, 1904, when Mary was 29, Daytona Educational and Industrial Training School for Negro

Girls opened. This title represented what she intended to accomplish: The girls' education would teach them how to live and how to earn a living. From the beginning, the school was nondenominational. The first enrollees were five girls between 8 and 12 whose mothers worked, and Bert Bethune. The tuition Mary hoped to collect was 50 cents a week, but inevitably there were times when even that was not forthcoming. Mary was determined to enlist the backing and cooperation of the Negro community, and she was successful in gaining it. As the school quickly increased its numbers, people contributed everything from labor to food. There was always the problem of paying for the meals the students ate during the day, and this was sometimes compounded with the necessity of boarding children when for one reason or another the mother was not available.

An excellent choir had helped Fiske University's recognition. Very soon Mary had trained her girls to sing spirituals, and she began to have them with her sometimes on speaking engagements that promoted the school. One who loved spirituals was John D. Rockefeller, and he became an enthusiastic benefactor of Daytona. Later the singing of Mary's school choir was an important factor in attracting the interest of Thomas H. White, president of the White Sewing Machine Company and manufacturer of automobiles known as White Steamers. White became the school's true friend and its most generous contributor. To add to Mary's joy, a woman presented her with a foot-pedal harmonium.

Daytona grew as a resort center. Mary's education-publicity campaign was beginning to reach beyond the town's limits. Black families in other parts of Florida were looking to send their daughters to Daytona as boarders. Mary saw that her school needed a permanent location rather than a rented one. She bought, deferring payment, a piece of land on the western edge of the black section. Known as Hell's Hole, it was a dump site, but she put her girls to work gradually removing the rubbish in preparation for building.

A board of sympathetic and influential citizens was now needed, and Mary set out to find the right people. Her sincerity and competence were decided assets in making a favorable impression on such persons. Also, she presented an air of confidence rather than deference and whenever possible showed her disdain of Florida's segregation laws by disregarding them. She persuaded James M. Gamble of Cincinnati's Procter and Gamble, along with the mayor of Daytona, a realtor, and two black ministers to become trustees. Gamble agreed to be chairman of the board and assumed the expense of having his lawyer attend to necessary details.

The year 1906 saw the building of Faith Hall, as it was to be called. By October 1907, it was possible to occupy the new building, though it was far from completed and sometimes construction stopped temporarily for lack of funds. The student body of about 100 moved in, prepared to make do with what was at hand and help with whatever presented itself.

With the missionary spirit that was part of her, Mary used the new facility on Sundays for what became known as Community Meetings for adults. These gatherings lent themselves to the interracial awareness that Mary encouraged. She also offered adults evening instruction in ways to make their lives a little easier. The same zeal prompted her to organize a school project called the Tomoka Mission to minister to the spiritual and other needs of Negroes of the area "turpentine" camps where conditions were deplorable. Through this, the students learned about community service. Five years after the Tomoka Mission began, Mary was instrumental in getting public-school authorities to provide education for the camp children for three months of the year. The Tomoka River was close to some of the camps; hence the project's name.

Mary's philosophy about educating blacks was in agreement with that of Booker T. Washington, who advocated, at that stage of their advancement, training to equip them for trades and vocations. She saw no shame in preparing girls to be first-class maids, and she saw the necessity of enabling them to cope with life in the white world. Some of the black community criticized this and supported the idea of William B.E. DuBois that Negroes should aim for the professions. Consistent with her beliefs, Mary had vegetables, strawberries, flowers, and sugarcane planted in the new location. Gardening was put on the curriculum, and much of the produce was sold to tourists. The girls were taught how to make syrup from the cane, and this syrup was used for home consumption. Each pupil put in some time every day working for the institution.

Mary was finding that her life was more and more focused on fundraising and organization. She bought a horse and buggy to get around in, abandoning the second-hand bicycle she had been using. She was also going to the North in search of financial support. In 1909, while on one of these trips, she met and persuaded Frances R. Keyser, a black graduate of Hunter College and a widow, to come South again and take over the educational program at Daytona, unfortunately at a pittance. Volunteers had been a great help in supplementing the efforts of the few paid teachers, but now the curriculum would be upgraded and developed systematically. The school had reached the level of grade B and had a new name—Daytona Educational Industrial Training School—because a few boys were admitted.

By 1911, McLeod Hospital, named in honor of Samuel and Patsy, was part of the school campus. It came into being when a student stricken with acute appendicitis had difficulty being admitted to a "white" hospital. The only one on the East Coast that admitted Negroes was in St. Augustine, run by the Florida East Coast Railroad for its employees. Beginning with a cottage that maintained two patient beds, the hospital became a 26-bed facility whose construction was financed largely by White and Gamble, with black people making contributions of their skills as well as money. McLeod accommodated persons not affiliated with the school, and it remained in existence until 1927 when the city of Daytona finally provided a hospital to serve its Negro population.

Daytona's first class to finish high school was graduated in 1915. To Mary's amazement and discouragement, the board had at first hesitated about the expediency of extending learning beyond the elementary level. She won by insisting that black youths were as entitled to education as white.

Faith Hall had become overcrowded, so in 1916 a much larger and versatile brick building was dedicated. It was named White Hall in honor of the school's great benefactor, who had died in 1914. He had left a bequest of $79,000. White Hall was distinguished by two posted mottos: *ENTER TO LEARN* and *DEPART TO SERVE.* By 1923, Mary's institution owned 20 acres with eight buildings and a farm, and the student body numbered around 300, the combined faculty and staff 25.

Most of the students were in the elementary grades, but as time went on, this type of instruction was terminated. There was a very real need for secondary education. By 1916, the South had still only about 65 public high schools for Negroes. Thus the high school department was continued until 1936. The Carnegie Foundation had made possible a collection of library books.

Such progress attested to Mary's vision, ability, and perseverance in a region where segregation and the Ku Klux Klan flourished. She had had the opportunity to tell her own story and her aspirations for the coming generations of her people to a Guggenheim, a Carnegie, a Mellon, a Vanderbilt, and many more. They had responded generously. The eminent Dr. Booker T. Washington and his entourage had visited Daytona and encouraged its mission. Some of the school's former pupils had advanced to become nurses, schoolteachers, owners of independent businesses, and so on. Two honorary degrees had been bestowed upon Mary McLeod Bethune.

When World War I started in Europe, the American Red Cross, which operated under a congressional charter, debated about whether Negroes should be allowed to participate in the organization's activities. Frederic Walcott, senator from Connecticut and a member of Daytona's board of trustees, was familiar with Mary's antisegregation views and her persuasiveness. Through him, she was invited to Washington to speak on the subject. She did so well that Red Cross officials sent her and three white women on a recruiting tour to Maryland, Virginia, and Pennsylvania. After that, the conflict ceased, and blacks were integrated into the organization. Later Thomas Marshall, Wilson's vice president and chairman of the Red

Cross, came south to attend a Red Cross rally at the school. His presence was a real morale lifter. Mary maintained contact with the Red Cross and used her organizational skills to direct rescue and cleanup operations in the aftermath of the killer hurricane that hit Florida in 1928.

Friends made it possible for Mary to tour Europe in 1924. Since her education was limited in scope, this was an opportunity for her to broaden her horizons.

Mary had long realized the risk involved in placing dependence on charitable donations. At the same time, she was vehemently opposed to asking aid from the state of Florida where bigots could and did exert great influence. The matter was resolved by a merger with Cookman Institute in Jacksonville, about 100 miles from Daytona. Founded in 1872 under the Freedmen's Bureau, Cookman had always educated Negro boys. It was run by the Methodist Episcopal church's Board of Education for Negroes. In 1925, Daytona deeded over all its property to the Methodist Episcopal Church to form Daytona Cookman Collegiate Institute, coeducational and open to white students as well as black. At the signing, Mary, then middle-aged, had this to say:

> It is a big thing to yield all. My feet are sore now, my limbs are tired, my mind weary. I have gone over hills and valleys, everywhere, begging for nickels and dimes that have paid for this soil, for these buildings, for this equipment that you find here. But, to the members of my Board, and to this organization that has come to take us, I want to bring it all this morning and cheerfully place it on the altar. I hold back nothing. But in doing this, in offering this resolution, in yielding my power, my personal power, my mental power, I am doing it with the confidence that you will never fail me. I yield it, Mr. Chairman, with God's blessing upon this work — with His sure protection around all we have done. Take it — develop it — use it.

She continued as president until 1942. In 1929, there was an official name change, to Bethune-Cookman College. The institution was accredited in 1936 as a junior college. Seven years later, the first four-year graduates received B.S. degrees in elementary education. Today "Mary's school" remains an independent accredited undergraduate college with a faculty of about 175 that serves close to 2,000 students.

As we have seen, Mary's activities were becoming more and more national in scope, in keeping with her views on civil rights. She was active in organizations such as the National Association for the Advancement of Colored People (NAACP), which in 1935 awarded her the Joel E. Spingarn Medal. Realizing that black women bore a double burden, she had a special interest in marshaling their influence. She was prominent in the National Association of Colored Women, focusing its efforts on fighting segregation and discrimination. She had also served on national committees during

Mary McLeod Bethune (no date). Courtesy of National Archives.

the Coolidge and Hoover administrations, but the presidency of Franklin Delano Roosevelt brought Mary a kind of second career, beginning with an appointment to the advisory board of the National Youth Administration.

During the Depression, the National Youth Administration (NYA) was set up to give part-time employment to students and provide training and employment to youths without jobs. Mary first met Roosevelt in 1935 when an appraisal was being made of the NYA's first year. She explained to him how much NYA checks meant to many young blacks in the South, how much the Negro needed equitable treatment. Urging the president's continuing assistance, she expressed the belief that now there was someone sympathetic in the White House.

In June 1936, Mary became the NYA's administrative assistant in charge of Negro Affairs. Three years later, her title was changed to Director, Division of Negro Affairs. Although she was still the nominal president of the college she had founded, her new position required most of her time and energy.

Her aim was to see that blacks received justice in the administration of NYA funds—a difficult task since the national office had little supervision over the state directors. She did have some success. She was a key figure in establishing a Negro college and graduate fund for those not otherwise receiving NYA funds. In this way, more than 4,000 received a total of $610,000 over a period of seven years. The NYA disbanded in 1944.

Mary had formed a warm friendship first with the president's mother, Sarah, and then with Eleanor, the first lady. Through the latter, Mary had the ear of the president. In 1938, she informed him as follows:

> The great masses of Negro workers are depressed and unprotected in the lowest levels of agriculture and domestic service while black workers in industry are generally barred from the unions and grossly discriminated against. The housing and living conditions of the Negro masses are sordid and unhealthy; they live in constant terror of the mob, generally shorn of their constitutionally guaranteed right of suffrage, and humiliated by the denial of civil liberties. The great masses of Negro youth are offered only one-fifteenth of the educational opportunity of the average American child.

Roosevelt thought so highly of Mary that after his death Mrs. Roosevelt made a gift to her of one of his canes (Mary had taken to collecting walking canes of famous men). Eleanor came to Florida to speak at the 35th anniversary of Mary's school and described it glowingly in her column, "My Day."

During World War II, Mary was temporarily released from the NYA to function as a civilian in the War Department to fight segregation in the armed services.

Following her formal resignation from the college's presidency and the termination of the NYA, Mary was almost as active as ever at fund-raising and working for causes dear to her heart. Her campus home in Daytona Beach, as it was now called, was named The Retreat. The guest book contained many famous names, among them Jane Addams, who had written, "This is a work after my own heart."

Many honors were bestowed on Mary. They included the Republic of Haiti's Medal of Honor and Merit (1949) and the Star of Africa, conferred by the Republic of Liberia in 1952. Of her 11 honorary degrees, perhaps the most significant was the one from Rollins College, a "white" Florida institution. She lived to enjoy six great-grandchildren and to rejoice over the 1954 Supreme Court Decision that declared all segregation in public schools "inherently unequal."

She died in 1955 at 79. In 1974, the U.S. government, in company with the National Council of Negro Women, dedicated the Mary McLeod Bethune Memorial Statue at Lincoln Park in Washington, D.C. The sculptor was Robert Berks. A 22-cent Mary Bethune stamp was issued in 1985.

Mary McLeod's enduring monument, Bethune-Cookman College, is also a monument to her philosophy of education—a philosophy exemplified by her lifework:

> Nature has stored up in individuals native powers, possibilities, potentialities, and it is the task of education to release these powers, to make actual and real these possibilities and potentialities in order that the individual himself may live to the fullest and make a contribution to the sum of total of human happiness. It means, further, that human happiness must be attained by the largest number of mankind finding harmonious adjustment within themselves and without, to the highest possible advantage.

Her "Last Will and Testament":

MY LAST WILL AND TESTAMENT—Mary McLeod Bethune

Sometimes I ask myself if I have any legacy to leave. My worldly possessions are few. Yet, my experiences have been rich. From them I have distilled principles and policies in which I firmly believe. Perhaps, in them there is something of value, So, as my life draws to a close, I will pass them on to Negroes everywhere in the hope that this philosophy may give them inspiration. Here, then is my legacy:

I LEAVE YOU LOVE. Injuries quickly forgotten quickly pass away. Personally and racially, our enemies must be forgiven. Our aim must be to create a world of fellowship and justice where no man's color or religion is held against him. "Love thy neighbor" is a precept which could transform the world if it were universally practiced. It connotes brotherhood and to me, brotherhood of man is the noblest concept of all human relationships. Loving your neighbor means being interracial, interreligious and international.

I LEAVE YOU HOPE. Yesterday, our ancestors endured the degradation of slavery, yet they retained their dignity. Today, we direct our economic and political strength toward winning a more abundant and secure life. Tomorrow, a new Negro, unhindered by race taboos and shackles, will benefit from this striving and struggling.

I LEAVE YOU A THIRST FOR EDUCATION. More and more, Negroes are taking full advantage of hard-won opportunities for learning, and the educational level of the Negro population is at its highest point in history. We are making greater use of the privileges inherent in living in a democracy. Now that the barriers are crumbling everywhere, the Negro in America must be ever vigilant lest his forces be marshalled behind wrong causes and undemocratic movements ... He must not lend his support to any group that seeks to subvert democracy.

I LEAVE YOU FAITH. Faith is the first factor in a life devoted to service. Without faith, nothing is possible. With it, nothing is impossible. Faith in God is the greatest power, but great faith too is faith in oneself. The faith of the American Negro in himself has grown immensely, and is still increasing. The measure of our progress as a race is in precise relation to the depth of the faith in our people held by our leaders.

I LEAVE YOU RACIAL DIGNITY. I want Negroes to maintain their human dignity at all costs. We, as Negroes, must recognize that we are the custodians as well as the heirs of a great civilization. As a race we have given something to the world, and for this we are proud and fully conscious of our place in the total picture of mankind's development.

I LEAVE YOU A DESIRE TO LIVE HARMONIOUSLY WITH YOUR FELLOW MEN. The problem of color is world wide, on every continent. I appeal to all to recognize their common problems, and unite to solve them. So often our difficulties have made us supersensitive and truculent. I want to see my people conduct themselves in all relationships, fully conscious of their responsibilities and deeply aware of their heritage. We are a minority of fifteen million living side by side with a white majority of 177 million. We must learn to deal with people positively and on an individual basis.

I LEAVE YOU FINALLY A RESPONSIBILITY TO OUR YOUNG PEOPLE. Our children must never lose their zeal for building a better world. They must not be discouraged from aspiring toward greatness, for they are to be leaders of tomorrow. We have a powerful potential in our youth, and we must have the courage to change old ideas and practices so that we may direct their power toward good ends.

Faith, courage, brotherhood, dignity, ambition, responsibility—these are needed today as never before. We must cultivate them and use them as tools for our task of completing the establishment of equality for the Negro. We must sharpen these tools in the struggle that faces us and find new ways of using them. The Freedom Gates are half a-jar. We must pry them fully open.

If I have a legacy to leave my people, it is my philosophy of living and serving. As I face tomorrow, I am content. I pray now that my philosophy may be helpful to those who share my vision of a world of Peace.

Juliette Gordon Low

At center stage in this chapter is a woman who represented privilege. She also knew sorrow, and from her pain the Girl Scout movement evolved.

Her father was William Washington Gordon, of Savannah, Georgia. A Yale graduate, he was a prosperous cotton broker, a partner in the firm of Tison and Gordon. Later he became sole owner. According to son Arthur Gordon, his father's watchwords were duty, courage, and loyalty. In line with this, William served for four years in the Confederate army, was wounded, and suffered the bitterness of defeat. His wife was Eleanor (Kinzie) Gordon, raised in Chicago when it was growing into a famous city. She too was educated in the East. Capable, witty, unconventional, and flamboyant, this good-looking woman impressed everyone who met her. She was also self-centered and devious. The couple had six children, of whom Juliette Magill Kinzie Gordon was the second, born in Savannah on October 31, 1860. Mrs. Gordon's correspondence made it clear that she did not want children—a futile complaint from a married woman in that pre–Sanger era. Daisy, as Juliette Low was known to her family, was devoted to her mother and loved her father dearly.

Daisy's birthplace was a beautiful Regency mansion, preserved today as a registered historical landmark and used as the Juliette Gordon Low Girl Scout National Center. As the Civil War went badly for the South, Savannah felt the pinch of insufficient food and supplies. Sherman's March to the Sea ended in Savannah on December 21, 1864. Previous to that, in April 1862, the Union general David Hunter had taken Fort Pulaski, located on an island near the mouth of the Savannah River, built to protect the city.

General Hunter was an uncle of Mrs. Gordon. He was particularly hated because he had freed the slaves in South Carolina, Georgia, and Florida (Department of the South, under his command) and then recruited them for the Union forces. For this he was officially reprimanded, but he was anticipating Lincoln's actions. Mrs. Gordon had three brothers who also fought for the North, one of them giving his life. Because of her connections, the despised General Sherman himself paid her a call. Such attention did not endear her to her Southern neighbors, despite the fact that her

Juliette Gordon Low birthplace, Savannah (courtesy of Library of Congress). This is now the Juliette Gordon Low Girl Scout National Center.

husband was ready to die for the Confederacy. When a Union military proclamation ordered the wives and children of Confederate officers to leave Savannah, Mrs. Gordon took her children by train to Chicago, where they stayed with the Kinzie family.

The Gordons returned to Georgia in August 1865. Although William had suffered serious financial losses, it appears that he slowly recouped his assets. Daisy's biographers speculate that Eleanor Gordon used some of her inheritance to help her husband. A stroke of luck was that the family home had suffered little vandalism. The Gordons were a close-knit family who enjoyed life and each other. As they were growing up, Daisy and two of her sisters spent their summers at Etowah Cliffs in northern Georgia where their aunt had a big house that sometimes accommodated as many as 20 young persons.

It was to Etowah Cliffs that William Gordon sent his family during the yellow-fever epidemic that hit Savannah in 1876. He refused to leave and prepared his will. Of course, it was not known then that this is a viral disease transmitted by a mosquito bite, and many of the so-called preventive measures were without scientific basis. Mr. Gordon tried to protect himself with a daily quinine pill and a drink of whiskey. He did not contract yellow fever and representing the Benevolent Association, did whatever he could do to relieve the suffering of the stricken and their families. When he died some 35 years later, Savannah's black newspaper noted that he had visited the black hospitals every day to be sure that their patients were not neglected. The rest of his family did not get the terrible disease.

Whereas Mary McLeod picked cotton, Daisy lived on its profits. She, like her sisters, was sent to private schools, first at home, then to boarding schools in Virginia and New York City. Painting and drawing were favorite subjects. She developed an appreciation of good literature, which is curious considering an inherent weakness in spelling that she never conquered. Some examples of her misspelling: *reccovered, vertuous, octabus, innocense, clept-imaniac.* "A dictionary is no use—half the time I don't even know how the word starts!" she once declared. She also became noted for her misuse of words. (She once accompanied Senator and Mrs. Oscar Underwood of Alabama to a White House reception and was responsible for having them introduced as Mr. and Mrs. Underbrush.) A letter from her literary and witty mother is an illustration of the family's unsuccessful attempts to instill correct usage: "Please remember that a person's *bust* means *both their bosoms* and according to your description of Alice's [younger sister] 'busts' the unfortunate child has four—two in front I suppose and two behind I conclude, which is certainly more than her share and I don't wonder her dress had to be let out."

We know something of Daisy as she was in her twenties. What we see presages the eccentric, noble person she would become. Besides the deficiencies mentioned, she was almost never on time; she was also scatterbrained and compulsive. On the positive side, she could show great enthusiasm. Her acts of kindness to all sorts of persons were somewhat unusual in someone her age. Along that line, she had a gift for making friends and entertaining them, especially in her home. She was a good swimmer; she was proficient at tennis and riding; she liked to act; she was a lover of animals. Photographs show a fine figure but a too-prominent pointed nose. A painting done by Edward Hughes about 1887 shows an attractive young woman with dreamy brown eyes and a gorgeous figure.

Now, more than a century later, it is difficult to envisage the sort of aimless life that Daisy lived for many years. Without children, vocation, profession, or the necessity to work, her life seems to have been filled with visits to friends and relatives near and far, with rounds of parties and other social events. Of course, in that Victorian-Edwardian age, she was financially dependent on her father at first and later on her husband. Mr. Gordon was adamant that no daughter of his was to travel by public transportation without an escort. Although he was willing to pay an escort, sometimes a suitable person was not easy to find, presenting a problem for the peripatetic Daisy.

In 1882, she made her first voyage to Europe. In England she visited with a family named Low. Andrew Low, the head of the house, was a multimillionaire, thanks to the cotton industry. He had lived in Savannah where he was friendly with William Gordon. They had been involved in some business operations and had connections through marriage, though not related. So it was natural that Daisy would contact the Low family, who had daughters. The heir to the Low family fortune was a handsome young man named William whose chief occupation in life seems to have been hunting, watching horse races, and other such inconsequential pursuits. He too was financially dependent on his father. Mr. Gordon had made it very clear that he did not regard a man born rich as a good suitor for his daughter; he much preferred one who had learned to support himself. When a romance developed between Daisy and Willy Low, it is not surprising that they kept it secret until they were sure they could marry with the approval of both fathers. Daisy paid a second visit to the Lows in 1884, and the following year Willy was in Savannah.

Daisy's marriage was one of the tragedies of her life. The second was her deafness. There is no certainty about the cause(s) of this. We do know from correspondence of her father that following an infection suffered in 1885 her hearing remained impaired on one side. Apparently it never improved but deteriorated over time. Some years later, when Mrs. Gordon inquired whether her daughter's hearing had improved, Daisy's comment was that she had great hopes of hearing Gabriel blow his trumpet on the day of judgment.

Andrew Low finally agreed to provide a settlement on his son, and William Gordon gave his consent to the marriage. However, Andrew died before the wedding took place, leaving his huge fortune to Willy.

The couple were married in Savannah in December 1886. Soon after the ceremony, Daisy developed pain in her good ear, supposedly due to an infection caused by a grain of rice thrown at the wedding. When healing took place, she was totally deaf on that side.

Willy had inherited a majestic mansion that occupied one of Savannah's city blocks. He had lived there when he was a small boy. While a guest there, Thackeray had written part of *The Virginians*. Robert E. Lee had paid a post–Civil War visit. This was of special interest to Daisy, who had a distinct admiration for the military. She always considered herself a Rebel, and ranked Lee very high on her list of heroes. She took great pains with redecorating, turning her new home into a very charming place. She seems to have been truly happy at this time.

The Lows had a life in Britain too. They rented a house in Leamington, and Willy took a 10-year lease on a grouse moor in Scotland while they looked about for something permanent. Daisy was accepted by Willy's relatives and friends and led the empty life of the idle rich. Soon she was presented at the court of Queen Victoria. There were parties, balls, the opera, sporting events, hunting, and so on, depending on the time of year.

By 1889, Willy had bought a home in Warwickshire. Wellesbourne House, as it was named, was not a castle or a manor house of the type inhabited by some of the Lows' friends, but it had huge stables. For Willy, the bigger, the better. Daisy loved to ride, but for some medical reason, that was soon forbidden her, much to her chagrin. She became very attached to Wellesbourne and enjoyed entertaining there. One of her projects was the construction of a pair of iron gates for the entrance. (Later these gates, with their daisy design, were removed to the entrance of Grandston Park, Savannah.)

In time, many of her own family came to visit at Wellesbourne. Mabel, a younger sister, met her future husband, an Englishman, when she was staying there. Once when Mrs. Gordon was a guest, she mentioned that an American related to her through adoption was married to an English author. When the relative was looked up, it was found that her husband was Kipling. He and his wife established a firm friendship with Daisy.

Both Daisy and Willy wanted children, but as the years went by, there were none. He began to spend more and more time hunting, sometimes in places far distant from England. Daisy often returned to Savannah with Mabel. She maintained close ties with her family and native land; she and her husband were spending less and less time together.

In the early days of her marriage, Daisy had written her mother about seeing a motto carved over a fireplace in an ancient house. The thought must have impressed her, for she had copied the motto:

Life is mostly froth and bubbles,
Two things stand like stone.
Kindness in another's troubles,
Courage in your own.

In her life of froth and bubbles, she would need courage.

The Spanish-American War was another excuse for her to return home in 1898. Just before she left, the Prince of Wales (later Edward VII) had been a luncheon guest at Wellesbourne. Mr. Gordon had volunteered his services and was commissioned a general. Mrs. Gordon was running a hospital in Miami for soldiers convalescing from typhoid fever, measles, and other medical disorders. Daisy joined her mother there and made herself useful making beef tea, broth, jellies, and such. When there was a milk shortage, she milked some cows herself until a pail was filled; apparently she had not forgotten everything she had learned years ago at Etowah Cliffs. Later she worked at a similar hospital in Pablo Beach.

Daisy had grown very close to Arthur, a younger brother, and to him she confided a little about her crumbling marriage. Actually, very little is known about what happened. According to her sister Mabel, Daisy had a collection of letters she wanted burned unread after she died. Arthur had charge of the family papers, and it is assumed that he complied with his sister's request. Also, no trace of a diary or journal has been found, and it is thought that Arthur disposed of this too.

In 1899, Daisy wrote Arthur, "I see so little of [Willy] I feel there is no human affection for me except in the family." Two years later, she told him, "Mama has tried not to say much to me, but I know she thinks if she was in my place she could manage Willy and engineer things much better than I do. But every heart knoweth its own bitterness and although I am sure there is much to be desired in my character, still I don't think anyone else can judge quite fairly."

A letter written in January 1901 to her sister Eleanor expresses some of the philosophy she must have evolved:

> But happiness is not the sum total of life. I am beginning to believe there is almost as much satisfaction in bearing pain bravely, as one grows older. One's own individual life is such a small part of the working of the big world; and if one lives up to the very highest level of one's powers, one can fulfill a tiny part of God's reasons in putting us here, and one's own affairs dwindle into supreme insignificance as compared with the scheme of existence as a whole—just as nobody counts the myriad little insects that die to make a coral reef and yet they have their uses and have not lived in vain.

During the summer of 1901, Daisy begged her sister Mabel, who was living in England, to come immediately to a home that Willy had in Scotland. When Mabel arrived, she found installed in the home of which Daisy should have been mistress an aggressive beautiful woman with whom Willy was obviously involved. This woman had taken over, ordering the servants about and arranging the living quarters to suit herself. Willy was showing only rudeness to his wife.

Apparently Daisy had known about the affair but had kept the information to herself until the situation had become intolerable. The two sisters returned to England, Daisy stopping at Wellesbourne for the last time to pick up her belongings. Later she set sail for Savannah.

She was 40, childless, now almost totally deaf at a time when hearing aids were not very effective, and according to Mabel, still in love with Willy. Even as late as the turn of the century, marriages were supposed to endure; divorce was the subject of gossip and often condemnation. Daisy's self-esteem is indicated by what she wrote with regard to the death of a friend's husband: "At least she can look back and know she made him happy, but I can only look back on failure."

Daisy went back to England prior to a divorce trial. Her family had rallied to support her morally and financially. Willy's sisters and friends

were sympathetic and helpful. Willy seems to have been mentally un-
balanced part of the time, which caused delays in the complicated and
drawn-out proceedings. He was drinking to excess, but whether this was
the sole cause of his symptoms is not known. He died suddenly in June
1905. As he had requested, his paramour made all the funeral arrangements. Daisy attended. A short time later, Willy's sister wrote to
Mabel that "dear Daisy has won the admiration of everyone by her quiet
dignity."

To cause Daisy added humiliation, Willy left nearly everything, including the Low house in Savannah and all of his American properties, to
his paramour. He provided for his wife by requesting that his mistress pay
Daisy £2,500 a year.

Daisy contested the will, which was settled in January 1906. She
received about $500,000 and the Low holdings in the United States.
"Sweet are the uses of adversity," she wrote her father, "for I can appreciate
the blessings I now enjoy, tenfold." Then she expressed appreciation for the
love and sympathy given her by her family, her lawyer, and "the host of
friends that have held out kind hands during the dark years I now hope are
over forever."

Daisy's life was as idle as ever. She remained bicontinental, shuttling
between Savannah and London where she bought a house; she also rented
a small place in Scotland; she visited India; she became eccentric.
Overgenerous to friends and those in trouble, she haggled over prices and
overdrew her bank balance. She bought a car and drove it with so little cau-
tion that she was a menace. She was known to invite friends to her home
and then forget that she had done so. Because of her deafness she devised
ways to dominate conversations by doing most of the talking herself.

In 1911, she met Robert Baden-Powell, who had founded the Boy
Scout movement three years previously. Baden-Powell, a military officer
and a bachelor, was a British hero because during the South African War
(1899–1902) he had successfully defended Mafeking for 217 days with
1,500 against an opposing force of 9,000 Boers. Later he resigned from the
army in order to devote himself full-time to scouting. In *The Character Factory* author Michael Rosenthal notes that scouting emphasizes "conservative virtues of conformity and obedience that would best generate the
continuation of the *status quo.*" He sees Baden-Powell as "an original, com-
pelling personality who gave the world its most distinctive youth organization, as well as a thoroughly indoctrinated exponent of imperial ideology
who articulated the prejudices and ideals of an incipiently crumbling empire." Regardless of Baden-Powell's motives, he had started a popular
movement that would have worldwide influence.

It was a mutual interest in sculpture that drew Daisy and Baden-
Powell together. He suggested she take lessons from Signor Lonteri, and

she followed his advice. Like Daisy, Baden-Powell could sketch, especially in watercolors, and had the unusal gift of being able to do it with either hand. He escorted Daisy (with a woman friend) to the coronation of George V, and although he was too busy for many social events, he did visit her home in Scotland.

During that visit, he must have piqued her interest in the British Girl Guides. A letter to her father is explanatory: "The Girl Guides is a sort of outcome of the Boy Scouts. When Baden-Powell first formed the Boy Scouts, six thousand girls registered as Scouts. And as he could not have girls traipsing over the country after his Boy Scouts, he got his sister, Agnes Baden-Powell, to form a society of Girl Guides. . . . I like girls and I like the organization and the rules and pastimes, so if you find that I get very deeply interested you must not be surprised."

Daisy found seven girls, who came to her home every Saturday afternoon. They lived in cottages scattered around that remote area. They learned the Guide Promise and laws, the history of the Union Jack, knot tying, knitting, cooking, and so on. Daisy was a firm believer in serving a delicious "tea." To provide an opportunity for the girls to earn a living without having to leave home for the city, she had them taught to raise chickens for nearby hunting lodges. She was in sheep country, so there was an abundance of wool. Capitalizing on this, she taught the girls to weave and found a London market for their products. Then she persuaded the postmistress of the village to run the spinning project after she left Scotland.

On Daisy's return to London, she continued her night class in sculpting. She also started two more troops of Guides—one in a basement that she hired in Fitzroy Square. In keeping with her contention that "the Guide laws are good for rich or poor," she centered the other troop in Lambeth, a disadvantaged area. Then she persuaded a friend to donate the use of a club room and find 20 girls to participate. Preparing for what would happen when she departed, Daisy approached Rose Kerr, who wrote about this later:

> "But," said I, "I cannot possibly do it. I have no time. I do not live in London. I am no good with girls."
> "Then it is settled," she said serenely, turning her deaf ear to me. "The next meeting is on Thursday and I have told them you will take it. I am sailing for America next week, but I shall be back in six months' time. I will pay for the girls' uniforms and other expenses you may be put to. And I should like you to give them a good tea every week after the meeting. Goodbye!" And she was gone, leaving me, not for the last time, gasping for breath!

It is amusing to note that a 1921 photo shows Rose Kerr in uniform at a Girl Guide rally held at Finsbury Park. Proficient in languages, she worked also to promote international guiding. A daughter, Alix Liddell, carried on these interests in the movement. Daisy's manner of dealing with Rose Kerr is typical of how she would operate. The results indicate that she possessed unusual judgment and persuasive powers.

On January 3, 1912, Daisy sailed on the S.S. *Arcadian,* bound for New York via the West Indies. Baden-Powell was also a passenger, scheduled to promote scouting in the United States as part of the world tour he was beginning. Aboard ship he met 22-year-old Olave Soames, whom he married before the year was out. In time, she supplanted Agnes Baden-Powell as head of the Girl Guides. We cannot know if Daisy, then 51, had regarded Baden-Powell, then 54, as a potential husband. But it is clear that his influence led her to found the Girl Scouts. For the rest of her life, she had a warm and friendly relationship with Robert and Olave Baden-Powell, known, respectively, as Chief Scout of the World and World Chief Guide.

By March 12, 1912, Daisy had 16 girls enrolled in two Savannah troops. The old carriage house and servant quarters of the Low home were now designated headquarters for the Girl Guides. Across the street, a basketball court and a tennis court were being constructed at Daisy's expense on a vacant lot that Daisy owned.

An article written for *Ms.* magazine in 1987 described the many changes in the Girl Scout uniform over 75 years. These first Guides of Daisy's wore middy blouses and long skirts made of dark-blue duck, square neckerchiefs of light-blue sateen, long black cotton stockings, and large black hair bows.

Before Daisy's next trip to England, she appointed Edith Johnson national secretary of the Girl Guides. Johnson's writings tell us much of the early progress of what is now the Girl Scouts of the United States:

> Like Mrs. Low's own enthusiasm, the enthusiasm of the girls for their Guiding spread about the city. Six troops were soon under way, some with six or seven members, others with as many as 60 or 70. When she left us, we followed her instructions and studied the English [Guide] handbook. . . .
>
> [Mrs. Low] wrote volumes to us, letters filled with quaintly misspelled words, and, whenever she heard of anything the English girls were doing that she thought we would enjoy, she at once dispatched a description of it to us.

That fall, Daisy was in mourning for her father. Referring to him in a letter to Arthur as "the only human being who was indulgent to my faults," she wrote, "He tried to make up to me for all that I lacked. He loved me no more than the others, but he knew I needed him more."

Back in Savannah in 1913, Daisy instituted day-camping for the Guides and took the first troop she had formed on a five-day camping trip. In addition, the first American handbook for Guides was issued.

Juliette Gordon Low about 1914. Courtesy of Juliette Gordon Low Girl Scout National Center.

Again Johnson is illuminating: "Already Mrs. Low's enthusiastic correspondence had awakened keen interest among her own friends, especially those in Washington, Boston, New York, and Cincinnati.... By this time the name had been changed to 'Girl Scouts.'"

In June Johnson went to Washington where Daisy wanted a national headquarters. "Each day some new person wrote saying she had heard of the Girl Scouts and wished to organize a troop," wrote Johnson. "I often wondered how they heard of us." She also noted that Daisy was supporting both the new headquarters and the Savannah organization as well as paying for patents, uniforms, handbooks, and other needs. The following year, she sold her pearls to meet expenses.

Daisy continued to expand scouting through relatives and especially the scores of friends she had made during her lifetime. Somehow she always managed to be put in contact with the appropriate person. After looking for recruits in New England, she went to Chicago in 1914. She stayed at Hull House where Jane Addams arranged for her to meet with important groups.

Though scouting was serious business, Daisy was still a madcap. She took a ride in a Deperdussin monoplane flown by a man who according to a seasoned aviator was "notorious as the pilot who takes the most risks." Later she rented a Scottish castle, supposedly haunted by a ghost. In time, she used the ghost story to amuse her Scouts.

The fear of German submarines did not deter Daisy's transatlantic crossings during World War I. In England, besides her Guide work, Daisy worked with Mabel in Belgian Relief. In 1916, Mrs. Gordon, then 80 and near the end of her life, wrote Mabel that Daisy had 7,000 Scouts registered. She also mentioned her daughter's unique spelling and added, "I do hope she will have no occasion to write any official notes unless she consults a dictionary."

Dictionary or not, Daisy was extraordinarily successful in spreading her cause. She moved the national headquarters from Washington to New York, where it is today. She set up a national New York council. One of the members of this council knew that Daisy was having difficulties in financing the organization from her own means and spearheaded a successful fund-raising drive. Very soon the Girl Scouts were on a sound financial basis.

This country's entry into the war gave the movement great impetus. The national board immediately wired President Wilson offering any help the Girl Scouts could give. Before the conflict was over, they had worked as units at Red Cross sewing rooms, helped at canteens in railway stations, planted vegetable gardens, and sold liberty bonds. When the influenza epidemic struck, they were on hand to release weary nurses for much needed rest.

By war's end, the Girl Scouts had their own magazine, *The Rally*, later named *The American Girl*, which was published until 1979. Nearly all the pictures taken as Daisy became famous show her in uniform. The garb was far from flattering, but she seems to have taken pride in wearing it. Olave Baden-Powell, visiting the United States with her husband, presented Daisy with the Silver Fish, the highest award bestowed by the British Girl Guides. Then Daisy's Scouts gave her a jeweled Thanks Badge, paid for with money collected from girls all over the country.

At the National Convention held in 1920, Daisy resigned, remaining known as the founder. She realized that her endeavor was secure and would continue to flourish without her. But her work did not stop; she devoted herself to the international aspect of Girl Scouting-Guiding, paying the expenses to attend world conferences of delegates from countries that could not finance their representatives. Rose Kerr, who ran Daisy's Lambeth Guide troop, recalled that Daisy's deafness made her a difficult committee member. "But with all this," Kerr wrote, "it was worthwhile to stop and listen to what she had to say, for her remarks were always illuminating. She was that rarest of human beings, an original thinker; she had a fresh, unbiased approach to any problem—besides unbounded courage." Daisy also had time to visit Scout rallies, troops, and camps. She liked to go on hikes with the girls, tell stories around campfires, and read palms. She took great interest in the making of a Girl Scout movie, *The Golden Eaglet.*

Daisy battled cancer toward the end of her life. She was most secretive about this last illness, so details are lacking. She kept her regular routine, never complaining. Her vagueness continued to the last. She suggested a Scout conference in Hawaii because it was so "central" to Central and South America. When reminded of Hawaii's position in the middle of the Pacific Ocean, she replied, "Maybe I meant Haiti. Why should we bother about minor details?" She died in Savannah in 1927 at 66 and was buried in the Scout uniform that in life she had been so eager to wear.

A World War II liberty ship was named for Daisy, and a three-cent postage stamp was issued in her honor in 1948. Today the Juliette Low World Friendship Fund promotes the Girl Scouts and Girl Guides throughout the world "as a contribution to peace and goodwill." Among its beneficiaries are four centers located in Mexico, England, Switzerland, and India.

When complimented on her success, Daisy's stock reply was, "The Girl Scout movement caught on because it was what girls wanted. The angel Gabriel himself couldn't have made them take it if they hadn't!"

True, but because of Juliette Gordon Low's understanding of girls and her dedication to them, the movement was there for them to take.

Girl Scouts of the U.S.A. currently has more than 3 million members, making it the largest voluntary organization for girls in the world today. Membership is open to any girl 5 through 17 who makes the Girl Scout Promise and accepts the Girl Scout Law. Minorities represent more than 13 percent of the total membership. Individual troops are organized by larger local units called councils, of which there are some 330, each chartered by the national organization.

Since its inception, Girl Scouts has changed in response to the changing interests and needs of girls. When the women's movement came into focus in the 1970s, former Scout Betty Friedan, whom we shall meet later, was invited to become a member of the national board. Serving on it from 1976 to 1982, she saw the organization "really evolve into a new consciousness of personhood, really prepare girls for leadership, in a way that isn't patronizing, doesn't infantilize real commitment to quality, real reaching out to black and white." Regardless of the programs offered, the commitment in helping girls to succeed has remained constant. The nation paid tribute to that commitment by issuing postage stamps in honor of the 50th and 75th anniversaries of the founding.

Since 1985, the organization has published booklets on contemporary issues: substance abuse; preventing child abuse; growing up female; preventing youth suicide; interesting girls in mathematics, science, and technology; facing family crises; preventing teenage pregnancy; critical environmental problems; prejudice, discrimination, and racism.

The Girl Scout national centers include the Low house in Savannah and the Edith Macy Conference Center near New York City. Some 706,000 adults, 99 percent of whom are volunteers, carry out the programs. Today troop leaders are not always the traditional models of the past. Sometimes they are young single women, sometimes college students, sometimes retirees of both sexes; anyone interested in girls is pressed into service.

Income is from a variety of sources—membership dues, sale of uniforms, unrestricted gifts, investments, and grants. At the local level, United Way is often a contributor; the sale of Girl Scout cookies generates a large percentage of funds.

The Girl Scout Promise
On my honor, I will try:
   To serve God and my country,
   To help people at all times,
   And to live by the Girl Scout Law.

The Girl Scout Law
I will do my best:
   to be honest
   to be fair
   to help where I am needed
   to be cheerful
   to be friendly and considerate
   to be a sister to every Girl Scout
   to respect authority
   to use resources wisely
   to protect and improve the world around me
   to show respect for myself and others through my words and actions.

Margaret Sanger

In the twentieth century, the most important factor in the liberation of women is the accessibility to contraception. The woman chiefly responsible for obtaining this accessibility is Margaret Sanger, whose story follows.

Her father was Michael Hennessy Higgins. Although born in Ireland, Higgins had been a drummer in the Civil War. Margaret was born in the factory town of Corning, New York, on September 14, 1879 (not in 1883, as she often claimed). Her father was a sculptor of marble and granite, earning commissions by carving such things as headstones. He was known among his friends as a free thinker, his agnosticism a far cry from his wife's Catholicism. Higgins was an advocate of socialism and took great interest in phrenology, a fad of the time that related the conformations of the skull to mental faculties and character traits.

Margaret's mother was Anne (Purcell) Higgins, a woman who was pregnant most of her married life. She delivered 11 children and had seven miscarriages. The frequent pregnancies did not improve her tuberculosis. Margaret was her sixth child.

The Higgins children were ostracized by the Catholic church because of their father's atheism. Margaret, thanks to her mother's efforts, was baptized and confirmed in the latter's religion, but without her father's knowledge. Nevertheless, all her life she considered herself an outsider to the church and as an advocate of birth control, carried on a running battle with the Catholic hierarchy.

Margaret, sometimes called Maggie or Peggy, received the equivalent of a high school education at Claverack College, a Methodist coeducational boarding school near Hudson in the Catskill Mountains. She earned her board and room by waiting on tables and washing dishes. Two older sisters who were working paid for her tuition and clothes.

Following three happy years at Claverack, Margaret tried teaching very young children at a public school in New Jersey and soon decided that teaching was not for her. Most of her pupils were the children of immigrants, and she had difficulty making herself understood. She had been there only a short time when she had to return to Corning where Anne Higgins was dying.

After her mother died, Margaret remained at home to help run the household. When she realized that her father was becoming almost a tyrant, she decided to leave.

Around the turn of the century, she was working at a new hospital in White Plains, New York. One biographer, Margaret Gray, states that despite the inferences in *Margaret Sanger, an Autobiography,* Margaret never received a diploma for nurse's training. Apparently she had some practical experience and was sincerely interested in obstetrics. It is clear from letters that she wanted a nurse's diploma and intended to work for one. However, a 29-year-old architect named William Sanger interfered with that plan.

There were similarities between Bill Sanger and Michael Higgins in that both eschewed organized religion, both believed in "radical" theories such as socialism, and both were impractical in their business dealings. Margaret and Bill were married in 1902.

Even before the wedding, Margaret had shown symptoms of tuberculosis. When she became pregnant, the disease flared up again. Bill sent her to a private sanitarium in the Adirondack Mountains. Run by Dr. Edward Trudeau, this institution offered the best treatment of the day, although rest and good nutrition were about all it offered (effective chemotherapy for tuberculosis was not available until the 1950s). Margaret was bored at Saranac Lakes and soon returned to New York City. Her first son, Stuart, was born in 1903 after a very difficult delivery. With another exacerbation of the disease, Margaret was forced to return to the sanitarium, where she remained for a year. There would be other flare-ups.

In 1905, Bill bought a plot of land in Hastings-on-Hudson and designed a house to build on it. He was a perfectionist, his ideas too expensive for his pocketbook. Margaret's illness had been costly and with the expenses of the house, he was in debt. Nevertheless, his considerable effort seems to have produced a structure worthy of the admiration of his contemporaries. The Sangers moved in in 1908.

That same year, a second son, Grant, was born. In 1911, there was a girl, named for Margaret but known as Peggy. Margaret loved her children but was always happy to have someone else look after them for her or to have them in good boarding schools.

When life in the suburbs became boring to her, she persuaded her husband to let them all return to New York where they rented a large apartment. The house that represented so much of Bill's creativity, that he called Margaret's Palace, went to the first person to make an offer. The price was low, and he should have waited. However, there was enough to pay the debts, and the mortgage payments paid over a period of years offered some security.

The new abode was a large apartment. Bill's mother, whom he

supported, moved in, providing Margaret with a built-in baby sitter. Living again in New York City, Bill had more time for his socialist activities. Margaret became interested, eventually meeting many people who influenced her thinking. Among them were labor leaders Eugene Debs and "Big Bill" Heywood; anarchist Emma Goldman, who wrote for *Mother Earth;* Emma's lover, Alexander Berkman, who had been imprisoned for attempting to assassinate an executive of the Carnegie Steel Company; Lincoln Steffens, the journalist, called a muckraker; Clarence Darrow, the lawyer with liberal ideas; John Reed, the radical journalist who later wrote an eyewitness account of the Bolshevik revolution; and Will Durant, who would author *The Story of Civilization.*

These people believed in social reform, some of them advocating violence if necessary to bring it about. It was a time when 20 percent of the population owned the nation's wealth, while 80 percent lived close to the edge of subsistence. As we mentioned at the beginning, benefits enjoyed today—social security and so on, as well as safe and healthy conditions in the workplace—were nonexistent. The unions were gaining strength but still lacked clout to bring about necessary legislation.

Margaret formally joined the Socialist Party's Local 5 and was paid to be an "organizer" of the Women's Committee. Her main task was to teach naturalization to the new immigrants crowding into New York. It was assumed that most of them would become Socialists.

The "organizer" job must have lost its glamour, for she soon quit. Then for a short time she worked for the Industrial Workers of the World. Known as the IWW or the Wobblies, this was an anticapitalist, anti-religious, anti–Old Glory organization. Its leader was Bill Heywood. When the textile mills in Lawrence, Massachusetts, were struck by the Wobblies, Margaret helped to evacuate strikers' hungry children to the homes of sympathetic volunteers in New York. Later she testified before a congressional committee about the deplorable conditions of these children. This would not be her only appearance before a congressional committee.

Through her sister Ethel, who was a nurse at New York's Mt. Sinai Hospital, Margaret sometimes found nursing opportunities. They usually involved deliveries in wealthy homes and infant care for a few weeks. With money scarce in the Sanger home, as it often was, such opportunities were most welcome. Soon Margaret began to work for the Henry House Visiting Nurses, mostly taking maternity cases. As we saw with regard to Lillian Wald, the clients were usually immigrants living in the Lower East Side. Margaret described in her autobiography the conditions she encountered, and they correspond well with what we presented.

It did not take long for her to realize that unwanted pregnancies could cause havoc in families already straining to make ends meet and that the

women were often determined that such pregnancies would be terminated.
According to her:

> Pregnancy was a chronic condition among the women of this class. Sug-
> gestions as to what to do for a girl who was "in trouble" or a married
> woman who was "caught" passed from mouth to mouth—herb teas, tur-
> pentine, steaming, rolling downstairs, inserting slippery elm, knitting
> needles, shoe-hooks. When they had word of a new remedy they hurried
> to a drug store.... They asked everybody and tried everything, but
> nothing did them any good. On Saturday nights I have seen groups of
> from fifty to one hundred with their shawls over their heads waiting out-
> side the office of a five-dollar abortionist.

The fate of a tenement woman, whom she called Sadie Sachs, changed
Margaret's life. Sachs, a Russian Jew, was 28. She had three children when
she found she was pregnant with a fourth. Jake, her husband, earned a
meager wage. Knowing that another mouth to feed would be a calamity,
she performed an abortion on herself. By the time a doctor was called and
then Margaret, Sadie had a blood infection. It was decided that she would
be taken care of at home. Food, ice, and other supplies had to be carried
up three flights and refuse and so on carried down three flights. To add to
the difficulties, a sizzling heat wave had settled on the city, making living
conditions in the Sachs quarters almost intolerable. But despite the absence
of antibiotics, after three weeks Sadie was well on the way to recovery.

When doctor and nurse were about to depart after a final visit, Sadie
wanted to know how to avoid having another baby. The doctor's response
was "Tell Jake to sleep on the roof." Convinced that Margaret had the
crucial knowledge, Sadie begged her to share it. Margaret knew only the
means used by the upper classes, use of the condom and withdrawal, and
assumed that a woman like Sadie wanted a method under female control.
But she did promise to come back later to talk with Sadie. She never did.

One evening three months later, Jake called Margaret again. Another
self-induced abortion, he said. Margaret took the subway to the tenement,
but Sadie died within ten minutes of her nurse's arrival. According to
Margaret,

> I left [Jake] pacing desperately back and forth, and for hours I myself
> walked and walked and walked through the hushed streets.... A moving
> picture rolled before my eyes with photographic clearness; women
> writhing in travail to bring forth little babies; the babies themselves naked
> and hungry, wrapped in newspapers to keep them from the cold; six-
> year-old children with pinched, pale, wrinkled faces, old in concentrated
> wretchedness, pushed into gray and fetid cellars, crouching on stone
> floors, their small scrawny hands scuttling through rags, making lamp
> shades, artificial flowers; white coffins, black coffins, coffins, coffins in-
> terminably passing in never-ending succession....

I knew I could not go back merely to keeping people alive.... I was resolved ... to do something to change the destiny of mothers whose miseries were vast as the sky.

Margaret's writings served as propaganda for her cause, and some critics think she often exaggerated to drive home her point. With regard to the above, historian James Reed has commented: "Whether or not Sadie Sachs actually existed, or her story represented a composite of several experiences, some of them perhaps borrowed from other nurses, is beyond proof. The abortion problem was real, and Sanger's portrayal of the attitude of physicians toward contraception was accurate, although there were a few doctors who argued that the poor wanted and could effectively use contraceptive information."

Some time would pass until Margaret could carry out her resolution. Meanwhile, various events in her life shaped the course she would pursue. About this time, Mabel Dodge, a socialite friend of Margaret's, described her as "a Madonna type of woman, with soft brown hair parted over a quiet brow, and crystal-clear brown eyes." Photographs show a slender, attractive woman.

Emma Goldman continued to impress Margaret. An advocate of free love, Emma described marriage as "a vicious institution which made women into sex-slaves just as capitalism made men into wage-slaves." She was a firm believer in what we now call birth control and routinely distributed leaflets on contraception at her lectures. These covered subjects as diverse as Shakespeare and the problems of women.

Margaret was in Provincetown, Massachusetts, a small town on Cape Cod, during the summer of 1913. Bill came from New York for weekends. By then, Margaret appeared to have accepted Emma's teachings, for she had a lover—the first of a number that included H.G. Wells. Bill had a liberal view on most issues but disagreed vehemently with Emma on this. When Margaret at a later date suggested that her husband find a mistress, he answered, "I still hold that intercourse is not to be classed with a square meal, to be taken at will, irrespective of the consequences."

Specific knowledge about contraception was essential to Margaret's plan for helping women. That summer she sometimes took the boat to Boston, leaving the children with a sister who was visiting. Even the Boston Public Library had none of the material she sought. She claimed that a library search lasting almost a year had been unproductive.

David Kennedy, in *Birth Control in America,* notes that in 1898 the index catalog of the Library of the Surgeon-General's Office listed nearly two full pages of books and articles on "prevention of conception." It discussed the condom, vaginal douching, suppositories, tampons, and the cervical pessary. Since the condom was a protection against venereal disease, physicians often recommended it for that purpose. If contraceptive information was readily available to the medical profession, it certainly was not to the general public. Later we shall see why this was so.

Soon the Sangers were planning a trip to France. Margaret would study contraceptive methods, and Bill would concentrate on painting, something he had yearned to do. They sailed for Europe in October 1913, a short time after the death of Bill's mother.

In Paris Margaret learned that druggists were selling suppositories containing spermicides, and she saw the rubber diaphragms that could be fitted over the uterine cervix to prevent pregnancy. She was impressed with the prevalence of small families. Bill met Matisse, Monet, and other painters, and was planning to stay at least six months. But Margaret decided that there was important work to be done in the States and surprised him by sailing for home after only one month. The end of the marriage was in sight, although there was not a formal divorce decree until 1921. Margaret explained it thus: "Sometimes in life the ideals which take possession of the mind become more imperious, more predominant than personal feelings. Such was the relationship between William Sanger and myself."

She had written articles on reproduction for a Socialist newspaper, the *Call*. They had been so well received that she was planning a publication of her own. Her series of sex-education articles for the *Call* had been in conflict with the so-called Comstock Law, and she knew there would be more trouble.

Anthony Comstock, born in 1844, held puritanical beliefs and conducted a lifelong crusade against pornography. He had been instrumental in obtaining passage of an 1873 bill that barred from the U.S. mail "obscene, lewd, lascivious, filthy and indecent" materials, which included contraceptive information and devices. The postmaster general named Comstock a special agent (later inspector), backed by the law to make arrests and confiscate contraband. Comstock did his job with the zeal of a fanatic. A master in the use of spies, decoy letters, false signatures, and the like, he estimated that over some 40 years he had brought about the destruction of 160 tons of obscene material. He also saw many persons convicted. The latter included physicians who had mailed contraceptive materials. The federal law had been inspired by New York State's strict one, and 18 states had passed "little Comstock Laws."

Printers were less than enthusiastic about doing the publication that Margaret had in mind. Finally one was found. Her radical friends helped her get advance subscriptions, and two affluent women made her loans (Bill was sending what money he could for the support of the family).

The *Woman Rebel* was launched in March 1914. According to an editorial, it would impart knowledge about the prevention of conception and other subjects. As time went by, articles attacked capitalism, criticized religion, and supported assassination. Abortion was mentioned, as was contraception, but without descriptions of actual techniques of the latter.

Margaret hoped that some of her writing would ultimately produce a showdown with Comstock—an opportunity to test the right of free speech. It was not long before she was notified by the Post Office that certain issues of her magazine were unmailable. Locals of the IWW managed to deliver copies, and some got by the postal authorities. However, disgruntled subscription holders made complaints about issues not received and the lack of information on how to avoid conception.

By August, the federal government had indicted Margaret for the publication of lewd and indecent articles, and worse, for incitement to murder and riot. She appeared in court without a lawyer and requested, with success, six weeks to prepare her case.

Instead of using the reprieve to fortify her position, she wrote a pamphlet, *Family Limitation*. It contained the information she had picked up in France, and she made it clear that diaphragms were not only expensive but had to be smuggled into the United States. (Rubber condoms, on the other hand, had been available in the United States before the Civil War.) Perhaps she had in mind some way to circumvent the law when she wrote, "Nurses and doctors will teach one how to adjust a diaphragm and women can teach each other." American nurses and doctors were not then prepared to do this, and lay gynecology was not practiced by women until some 50 years later. Many printers shunned the project, one calling it a Sing Sing job. Finally a brave Wobblie named Bill Shatoff agreed to do it after hours. Margaret could afford an order of only 100,000 copies but intended to have more run off later.

With no defense prepared, she asked for another extension. She was allowed eight days and a small bail. When she sought competent legal advice, she learned that little could be done for her. Margaret made a decision to jump bail and go to England. After making sure than her children would be cared for, she armed herself with letters of introduction to Europeans who could help her and boarded a train for Canada. From the train she wrote to court officials that she was leaving the country under an assumed name (she was extraditable) and would return when better prepared to plead her case.

In Canada friends obtained a forged passport for her, enabling her to sail to Liverpool on November 3, 1914. Before her departure, she had a brief visit from her husband. World War I had forced Bill to leave France. His financial situation was so desperate, he had to borrow to pay for a steerage passage home. Apparently he wanted to continue the marriage.

From the ship Margaret sent coded cables to various IWW locals, from the wool factories of New England to the coal mines of West Virginia, about distributing *Family Limitation*. Eventually 10 million copies were

Margaret Sanger in London, 1916. Courtesy of Sophia Smith Collection, Smith College.

sold and translated into many foreign languages. Margaret had now begun in earnest to carry out the vow she made when she saw Sadie Sachs die, and the effort would become her singular mission. In a very short time, her writings and actions would keep her and the birth-control movement in the public eye.

Why she did not use the title *Birth Control* rather than *Family Limitation* is puzzling. The former term was coined by a man named Robert Parker. It is usually attributed to Margaret, but according to Parker, "I may have coined the words, but Margaret passed them around the world. Without her, birth control would never have become household words."

Margaret spent almost a year abroad. She met leaders of the British birth-control movement, including Marie Stopes, who later founded England's first birth-control clinic. Margaret was heartened to learn than an 1876 court decision had established that in that country contraception was not an obscenity. She met Havelock Ellis, the distinguished psychologist and author, and began an association that lasted until he died. Ellis encouraged her to study widely, and in so doing she gained a broad perspective of the issue of birth control. She made many friends in England and would return for more visits.

Holland had had government-sponsored birth-control clinics for years, and she was able to visit one at The Hague. Here she was shown a diaphragm invented by a physician named Mensigna. Recognizing that it was superior to what she had seen in France, she learned how to fit it. At that point, Margaret changed her mind about lay gynecology, deciding that it was not a good idea. In the years ahead, much of her effort was expended in making the medical profession receptive to birth control.

Back home, Bill was in prison because he had been tricked by one of Comstock's decoys into giving away a copy of *Family Limitation*. Comstock, who died soon afterward, made the arrest himself, announcing to the press that the author was "a heinous criminal who sought to turn every home into a brothel."

Soon after Margaret's return to New York, her daughter developed pneumonia and died. When Margaret appeared in court to face the charges that she had dodged, there was much sympathy for the devastated mother. The National Birth Control League, formed during her absence, rallied to her defense. Socialist groups all over the country had also contributed, and various personalities had made known their support. Not wishing to make a martyr of Margaret Sanger, the government in February 1916 entered *nolle prosequi*.

Margaret's activities on behalf of her cause required money. From the beginning, she was fortunate in being able to attract wealthy and influential people who were willing to donate. With her sons in boarding school, she toured the country, delivering a basic speech on birth control. In one year, she would deliver this 119 times. Some states were more permissive than others about allowing the distribution of contraceptive materials. She was arrested and jailed in Portland, Oregon, for selling *Family Limitation* but given a suspended sentence. Through the intervention of the Catholic church she was prevented from speaking in St. Louis. She capitalized on such actions, declaring, "I see immense advantages in being gagged. It silences me, but it makes millions of others talk about me, and the cause for which I live." The tour made her better known and gave her valuable experience as a national organizer.

She was now resolved to open a birth-control clinic—a deed that some consider her single greatest contribution. Although Comstock had died, his influence lingered on; since anything pertaining to contraception could not be handled in the mail. Worse still, according to Section 1142 of the Penal Code of New York State, it was a misdemeanor to give away or sell any information on the subject. Section 1145 held a ray of hope for Margaret; because it allowed a physician to prescribe contraceptives for the cure or prevention of disease, she thought that a liberal judge might apply it to any situation when pregnancy could be said to jeopardize a woman's health. She believed that if starting the clinic resulted in her arrest, she would have an opportunity to test the interpretation of Section 1145. Margaret was aware that Emma Goldman had been sent to the workhouse for merely speaking publicly about birth control, but this did not deter her plans.

The site chosen was a crowded tenement in the Brownsville section of Brooklyn. Unsuccessful in finding a physician, Margaret decided that she and her sister, Ethel Byrne, who was a trained nurse, would teach about contraception. They would explain the use of diaphragms but make no actual fittings. For those who wanted them, the correct size would be estimated from the number of births and miscarriages. Douches and condoms would be discussed. Histories and records would be kept by Fania Mindell, a young Russian Jew from Chicago who had been attracted to the cause on Margaret's recent lecture tour. Five thousand handbills in English, Yiddish, and Italian were printed on credit and widely distributed. In retrospect, we note that all who were in any way connected with the project showed real courage.

The clinic opened on October 16, 1916, serving 140 women the first day. The next day there were articles about it in various newspapers. Within a week, women were coming from Connecticut, Massachusetts, and New Jersey. Many who lived at a distance and were unable to come requested information in the mail. One woman was a decoy for the vice squad, and on October 26 the operation was shut down. Margaret, Fania, and Ethel were arrested and the literature and supplies seized. The women were not jailed while they waited for separate trials. Margaret tried to reopen the clinic so popular with poor women, but the police prevailed.

The sisters were charged under Section 1142 for distributing contraceptive devices and Fania for giving out obscene literature in the form of a booklet called *What Every Girl Should Know*. This was reprinted from Margaret's articles in the *Call*.

In January 1917, Ethel was sentenced to 30 days on Blackwell's Island. Following the example of the British suffragettes, she went on a hunger strike, with Margaret ably directing news releases. The national press made the most of it when Ethel was forcibly fed. In addition, Margaret's supporters staged a giant protest meeting at Carnegie Hall. As public criticism continued to mount, New York's Governor Charles Whitman released the nurse with Margaret's promise that her sister would not return to the movement. Franklin P. Adams of the *New York Tribune* wrote, "It will be hard to make the youth of 1967 believe that in 1917 a woman was imprisoned for doing what Mrs. Byrne did."

Fania received a fine of $50, which was paid by Mrs. Amos Pinchot, a friend of birth control who was generous with her money.

Refusing a fine, Margaret was given 30 days in jail, which she spent at a Long Island penitentiary where the facilities were at least adequate and clean. She refused freedom for the promise not to repeat the offense.

Her lawyer was Jonah Goldstein, who had as a youth been influenced by Lillian Wald, and he appealed both Margaret's case and Fania's. The decree on the latter was overturned. In January 1918, Judge Frederick E. Crane, of the Appellate Division of the New York Supreme Court, ruled that Margaret's conviction be upheld because only a physician was covered by the law's exemption (Section 1145). However, as Margaret had foreseen could happen, he interpreted "prevention of disease" in a broad sense. Whereas the original intent was to protect males from venereal disease, the law could now protect women against pregnancy.

The *Birth Control Review* was begun by Margaret in 1917. A propaganda vehicle, it offered articles on child labor, eugenics, demography, the legal aspects of birth control, and so on.

The coeditor was Frederick Blossom, a Socialist who also did fundraising. There was friction between him and Margaret, and he quit suddenly, taking with him office furniture, subscriber lists, account books, and the like. Margaret, still a member of the Socialist Party, reported him to the district attorney. In so doing she alienated the IWW by going to "an outside agency—the capitalistic district attorney." The New York Birth Control League had been organized by Blossom, and now its more radical members turned against Margaret. She was also at odds with the National Birth Control League because she did not approve of its leader, Mary Ware Dennett. Claiming the expression *birth control* was hers, Margaret soon forced the organization to change its name to the Voluntary Parenthood League.

It was time for Margaret to take stock of sources of badly needed support. She came to the conclusion that although the working classes had been of immeasurable help to her and had been her primary concern, ironically, her ideas were not in tune with theirs. For instance, she did not agree when she heard her friend Bill Heywood tell the Wobblies that it would be a great achievement when people became rich enough to have all the babies they pleased. Nor did she agree with former president Theodore Roosevelt when he deplored race suicide of the Anglo-Saxon segment of the U.S. population. Her contention was that *all* women should be freed of frequent childbearing. Children should be well spaced, and every child wanted.

Margaret did not hold the view of many religious people that sex was only for the procreation of children. She regarded it as something that should bring pleasure to both partners without creating unwanted pregnancy. She expressed her philosophy well in a 1921 speech:

> The law requires a married woman to give of herself to her husband or forego his support. This makes self-control by women impractical, if not impossible . . . and the argument that the use of the marriage relationship is only for the purpose of procreation would conceivably have to limit unions to only a few times in the course of a marriage. . . . This last is perfectly absurd because it places man on the same level as animals. . . . There is another side, another use of the marriage relationship. I contend it is just as sacred and beautiful for two people to express their love when they have no intention of being parents.

She realized that since birth control was more accessible to the upper and middle classes and more acceptable to them, she would do well to concentrate on gaining the support of the wealthy; with education, the poor would in time change their attitude.

Margaret had proven herself a successful speaker; she was soon a successful author, and both activities were lucrative for her. *Women and the New Race* came out in 1920, followed by six more books of which she was author or coauthor. She was especially fortunate in finding expert editorial assistance.

She was divorced in 1921. Bill had written, "As to keeping my name after a possible re-marriage, certainly you can. In fact I am proud to have been married to a woman who carried that name so high."

Margaret became very adept at organizing large conferences. Just before the opening in New York of a three-day conference on birth control, she announced the formation of a new organization, the American Birth Control League. The conference drew 1,000 physicians. On the third day, the featured speaker was prevented from delivering his talk because Catholic officials exerted pressure on the police to prevent him from speaking. But the resulting publicity benefitted the birth-control movement.

By this time, Margaret had met J. Noah Slee, millionaire president of the Three-in-One Oil Company. Although he was about 20 years her senior, she was toying with the idea of marrying him. After parting from Bill, she had rejected marriage proposals from younger men, seemingly because dedication to her cause was an overriding factor in her life. Moreover, she regarded marriage as legalized prostitution. Slee was receptive to her cause, so perhaps marriage to him was more tempting when she was sure it would mean a substantial source of funds for the birth-control movement.

Japan was experiencing some very serious population problems, and in 1922, the Kaizo (Young Reconstruction League) of Japan contracted for Margaret to deliver eight or so five-hour lectures. Sailing from San Francisco, she took son Grant with her on what would be a global journey. Noah Slee was on the same ship. Margaret's addresses received exceptionally good press coverage. The trip included other parts of the Orient—Korea, China, and Hong Kong. She was able to participate in the Fifth International Neo-Malthusian and Birth Control Conference in London.

Margaret was interested in this conference because her viewpoint was international, not parochial, and she was ahead of her time in recognizing the dangers of overpopulation. During World War I, she had made known her dedication to pacifism. Now she was alarmed that Japan, Germany, and Italy were pleading with their women to bear more children; when these countries became too crowded at home, they could claim the right of expansion. Thus she hoped that nations would limit their populations according to their resources as a fundamental principle of international peace. (Later, Planned Parenthood would commit itself to achieving through informed individual choice a population of stable size in an optimum environment.) She left the conference with the expectation that the next such one would be held in the United States.

Slee's marriage to Margaret was not discovered until 1924. The wedding had taken place in London two years earlier. Presumably it had been kept quiet since both were divorced. Margaret had demanded a signed agreement giving her complete independence. She would have her own apartment and servants within Noah's home, with the door kept locked. When he wanted to see her, he was to telephone.

Throughout their life together, Noah provided very well for Margaret and her sons. He gave generously to the American Birth Control League and offered that organization business acumen and managerial skills that Margaret was sometimes not inclined to take. In 1928 she resigned from the League she had founded because she disagreed with some members of its board. Her devotion to the cause remained, and her husband continued to donate to that cause.

When the couple was settled in New York after the world tour, Margaret started a birth-control clinic she intended to be permanent. As we have seen, the law now permitted a physician to prescribe a contraceptive for a woman whose health would be impaired by childbearing. For a while this idea dominated the clinic. After Dr. Hannah Stone was hired, women who wanted diaphragms for social reasons were accommodated. Dr. Stone coauthored with her gynecologist husband a very popular book, *Marriage Manual,* and her tenure at the clinic did much to enhance its reputation.

Noah purchased a brownstone near Fifth Avenue that soon became the new home of the clinic, now named the Margaret Sanger Clinical Research Bureau. As the patient load increased, a major problem was to provide sufficient diaphragms. Noah came to the rescue by having them smuggled into the country through his Three-in-One Oil Company. He also provided money to develop future domestic production of diaphragms.

Margaret came to the realization that her movement and clinic really needed strong support from the medical profession. With this in view, she hired Dr. James Cooper, a gynecologist and former medical missionary, to educate doctors about birth control. In general, the medical profession was prepared to use contraception as a health measure; there was less enthusiasm when it was considered a social measure, and this is what Margaret emphasized. In addition, very little research had been done about the efficacy of various methods, another problem that Margaret hoped her clinic could address with good record keeping. Over a period of two years, Dr. Cooper visited all the states in the union, addressing county medical societies and acquainting them with the latest information. It was a highly successful project. With Dr. Stone, Dr. Cooper found how to make a cheap contraceptive paste containing lactic acid; its use with the diaphragm increased the effectiveness of the latter.

When the clinic was raided, again at the instigation of the Catholic church, a medical authority who was making an investigation found the clinic "quite in keeping with the spirit and purpose of the law and with the spirit of medicine, public health medicine." In fact, the clinic became so well thought of that soon about 50 modeled on it were scattered about the country.

Zurich was chosen by Margaret for the 1930 Seventh International Birth Control Conference, which she organized. For five days 130 clinic directors and scientists exchanged ideas. Here it became clear that in most parts of the globe, the concept of birth control was slowly taking hold.

In the nineteenth century, a very crude method of estimating a "safe period" for intercourse had been worked out. In 1933, "rhythm" appeared, reflecting better knowledge of the menstrual cycle. This birth-control method is based on the fact that if intercourse is omitted during a period when the ovum can be fertilized, pregnancy will be prevented. The difficulty is to determine when ovulation has taken place, and in reality there is no "safe time." Since no mechanical device was involved, the Catholic church approved the rhythm method. This was an advance because it undoubtedly prevented some pregnancies and contradicted the idea that intercourse is solely for the procreation of children.

Opposite: **Margaret Sanger (right) at booth of National Committee on Federal Legislation for Birth Control (192?). Courtesy of Library of Congress.**

The year 1935 saw Margaret in India. She met with Gandhi, who believed in birth control but advocated abstinence to obtain it. Men wanted sons for security, and she realized that a massive educational effort would be needed to change attitudes in a country so overpopulated.

Two years later, there was real progress on the home front. In 1935, the government had seized a package of contraceptives sent to Dr. Hannah Stone from Japan. The confiscation was justified on the basis of Section 305 of the Revenue Act, which barred importation of articles preventing conception. When the seizure was challenged, Judge Grover Moscowitz ruled that Section 305 could not stop the importation of articles preventing conception. When the government appealed this decision, Judge Augustus Hand of the circuit court of appeals upheld the opinion, adding that Section 305 and similar statutes had a common origin in the Comstock Law. Morris Ernst, an attorney involved in the victory, made it clear to the American Medical Association (AMA) that the decision applied to all states except Connecticut and Massachusetts, which had their own local laws about birth control.

Margaret was overjoyed when in 1937 the AMA made a full endorsement of birth control, declaring, "Voluntary family limitation is dependent largely on the judgment and wishes of individual parents." Dr. Robert L. Dickinson, the eminent gynecologist who had fought for ten years for enlightened thinking in his profession, telegraphed, "Amongst foremost health measures originating or developing outside of the medical profession, Margaret Sanger's world wide service holds high rank and is destined eventually to fullest medical recognition."

The American Birth Control League found that it needed the name of Sanger, which it had lacked for 10 years. In 1938, the group merged with Margaret's Clinical Research Bureau to form the Birth Control Federation of America, with a physician president. The name was changed in 1939 to Planned Parenthood Federation of America, with Margaret Sanger as honorary president.

When she became less active, she moved from New York to Tucson, Arizona. Noah died in 1942. Margaret continued her work as long as her health permitted. Both her sons became physicians, and she took great interest in her grandchildren. In 1952, she made repeat visits to Japan and India. Always seeking technological advances in contraception, she persuaded her friend Kate Dexter McCormick to provide money for Gregory Pincus of the Worcester Foundation for Experimental Biology in Massachusetts to do research that resulted in the anovulatory pill.

Beginning with the Medal of Achievement from the American Women's Association in 1931, Margaret received the honors due her. In 1949, Smith College conferred an honorary degree. Two years later, she was awarded the Lasker Award, a prize of $1,000, for outstanding achievement in a field connected with medicine. There have been television versions of her life.

During her last years, she was beset with serious medical problems, and she developed an addiction to the drug Demerol. She died in 1966, one year after the U.S. Supreme Court had declared unconstitutional a Connecticut law forbidding married couples from using contraceptives. The suit had been brought by Planned Parenthood.

Although Margaret Sanger was a woman of unusual ability and vision, her work is deplored in some quarters. For example, Elasah Drogin, whose viewpoint is pro-life, has written an extremely critical book entitled *Margaret Sanger, Father of Modern Society*. In it she claims that Margaret's writings promoted enforced sterilization of the "unfit," abortion, racism, genocide, and so on—ideas that according to Drogin, are especially lamentable because their influence is with us today. It is true that eugenics, which deals with the improvement of hereditary qualities by social control of human reproduction, was very popular in the 1920s, and there were in the birth-control movement people who believed in enforced sterilization of the "unfit." As to enforced sterilization and abortion today, Planned Parenthood is dedicated to reproductive *choice*. The organization's response to some of the anti–Sanger charges of the type made by Drogin appears in a 1985 paper authored by Charles Valenza.

Robert G. Weisbord, in his 1975 book, *Genocide? Birth Control and the Black American*, finds Margaret's "flirtation with eugenics and nativism [policy of favoring the native inhabitants of a country as against immigrants]" a "blot on her movement's otherwise excellent record." He regards the charge of genocide against blacks groundless. If Margaret did have racist ideas, it should be noted that in recent years, one of Planned Parenthood's most flamboyant presidents has been a black woman, Faye Wattleton.

Often Margaret's actions were not commendable. For example, since she intended to be the leading light in the birth-control movement, she did not hesitate to denigrate the work of two other worthy workers, Marie Stopes of England, and Mary Ware Dennett, one of the founders of the first birth-control league in this country. Whether this was done for the good of the cause or to keep her position secure is not known.

In any case, her effort to make birth control accessible to all who want it remains a singular achievement. Grant Sanger was impressed with his mother's utmost concentration on the problem. "From the time she started the business until she finished, she never deviated," he noted, "Not into woman's suffrage, not into the labor movement, not into anything. She always stayed right with it. Her entire life was devoted to it."

It is tempting to speculate about Margaret's opinions if she lived today. She would certainly prefer the current attitude toward sex compared to that which existed when the U.S. Post Office declared her "What Every Girl Should Know" article on venereal disease for the *Call* too obscene to be printed.

She would undoubtedly be proud that Planned Parenthood has birth-control clinics throughout the nation, providing leadership in making effective means of voluntary fertility regulation accessible to all. This includes contraception, abortion, sterilization, and infertility services. Relevant biomedical, socioeconomic, and demographic research is encouraged. She would likely demand more educational programs in an attempt to reduce the number of teenage pregnancies. No doubt she would hail Planned Parenthood's acceptance of Norplant®, the long-acting female contraceptive approved in 1990 by the FDA.

The International Planned Parenthood Federation is active in many nations. As infant mortality decreases in the developing nations, parents become more receptive to the idea of limiting the size of their families. We assume that Margaret would rejoice because of changed attitudes and see that all possible aid goes to these countries.

What Margaret's stand on abortion would be is debatable. She pleaded for legal contraception as a means to avoid abortion. However, at that time, hemorrhage and infection were common life-threatening complications of abortion, making the procedure less safe than it is today. On the other hand, in the 1930s, Margaret's wish was that clinic patients who had missed a menstrual period should receive counseling from a physician who had "contact with hospitals or doctors who may, in therapeutic cases, give proper attention to those coming under that term." Planned Parenthood is committed to the continuation of the 1973 Supreme Court decision that made early abortion legal—the right of a woman to choose whether to terminate an unwanted pregnancy. It appears that Margaret would agree with this, supporting abortion for social as well as medical reasons. "No woman can call herself free," she declared, "until she can consciously choose whether she will or will not be a mother." It also appears that she would approve of the use in early pregnancies of the abortifacient drug RU 486, developed by France's Etienne-Emile Baulieu. Dr. Baulieu was awarded Planned Parenthood's 1989 Wippman Scientific Research Award.

Much has been said in praise of Margaret Sanger. A Unitarian minister who heard her speak at Carnegie Hall when her sister was in jail wrote one of the best compliments:

> I never saw anything like it. It had the spirit of the abolition days. Margaret took the audience and lifted it up. She had dignity. She had power. You can tell in five minutes whether a person is an actor or has the real secret of power. She had it—the power of a saint combined with the mind of a statesman. I realized that night she was one of the great women of our time.

Carrie Chapman Catt

How women won the vote has been described as follows:

To get that word, male, out of the Constitution, cost the women of this country fifty-two years of pauseless campaign; 56 state referendum campaigns; 480 legislative campaigns to get state suffrage amendments submitted; 47 state constitutional convention campaigns; 277 state party convention campaigns; 30 national party convention campaigns to get suffrage planks in the party platforms; 19 campaigns with 19 successive Congresses to get the federal amendment submitted, and the final ratification campaign. Millions of dollars were raised, mostly in small sums, and spent with economic care. Hundreds of women gave the accumulated possibilities of an entire lifetime, thousands gave years of their lives, hundreds of thousands gave constant interest and such aid as they could.

The above was written by Carrie Chapman Catt. Although she stood on the shoulders of giants, the Nineteenth Amendment is an enduring monument to her. She also founded the League of Women Voters.

Her parents, Lucius Lane and Marie (Clinton) Lane, were of English stock. Of their three children, Carrie was the second, born January 9, 1859, in Ripon, Wisconsin. After the Civil War, the Lanes moved farther west to a new farm near Charles City, Iowa.

According to Catt biographer Mary Gray Peck, Carrie was shocked to learn that her mother could not vote in the 1872 presidential election (Grant versus Greeley), and the knowledge made a deep impression on the 13-year-old.

Carrie attended high school in Charles City, riding five miles each way on horseback for part of the year. During the winter months, she boarded in town with family friends. After finishing in three years, she taught for a year at the local district school. Around this time, she read *The Origin of Species,* and Darwin made a lasting impact on her thinking.

The year 1877 saw Carrie in Ames at the Iowa State College, then considered a center of liberal thought, perhaps because evolution was discussed in many courses. Carrie was earning her way and obtained a job as assistant librarian at ten cents an hour. She used this to advantage to become a speed reader, concentrating on nonfiction. During her college career, she also made an extensive study of the works of Herbert Spencer, to whom the concept of Social Darwinism is attributed. She was awarded a bachelor of science degree in the fall of 1880.

With the intention of entering law school, Carrie spent the next year in the office of a Charles City lawyer. When offered the principalship of the high school in Mason City, she took it, intending to save most of her salary for law-school expenses. Eighteen months later, when the school super-intendent resigned, Carrie was appointed to replace him. She appears to have abandoned her earlier ambition for a career in law once she was earn-ing a good living.

Carrie resigned in 1884 at the end of the school year. She had fallen in love with Leo Chapman, editor and owner of the *Mason City Republican*. They were married in February 1885. Without school duties, she became assistant editor of her husband's paper. That year she attended a conven-tion of the American Woman Suffrage Association in Cedar Rapids and there met Lucy Stone, the noted reformer and suffragist. In 1886, the *Mason City Republican* was sold, and that summer Chapman went to the West Coast with the intent of buying another newspaper. When he con-tracted typhoid fever, his wife started immediately for San Francisco, but he died while she was on the way.

After working a year for a San Francisco newspaper, Carrie returned to Charles City. She began to lecture for a fee ranging from $10 to $25, but when the Iowa Woman Suffrage Association contacted her, she agreed to become its state organizer, with only her expenses paid. Getting the vote for women seems to have become an inner compulsion and would occupy the next 33 years of her life.

We digress here to look at the background of the suffragist movement in the United States.

As educational opportunities improved for women, their demand for equal rights with men intensified. Some state laws had contributed to the advancement of women, but by mid–nineteenth century, there was still much to be gained. For instance, by 1850, almost 24 percent of the work force were women, and reform in wages and working conditions was urgent.

At the women's-rights convention held at Seneca Falls, New York, in 1848, there was sufficient demand for political equality to pass a resolution declaring it was "the duty of the women of this country to secure for themselves their sacred right to elective franchise." The conference had been called by Lucretia Mott and Elizabeth Cady Stanton, both of whom had been excluded eight years earlier in London from the World Anti-Slavery Convention, where it was ruled that only men would be seated.

The Seneca Falls convention inspired women to organize. Susan B. Anthony soon joined the movement and became through her organizational ability and indefatigable efforts the best-known figure in the suffragist forces. Stanton, with whom Anthony formed a lasting bond, was particularly interested in reforming the divorce laws, an educated electorate, and criticizing passages in the Old Testament that were derogatory to women. The latter interest developed because the church was largely opposed to measures that contributed to female liberation. The group used to advantage Lucy Stone's gift of oratory that was so effective in antislavery campaigns. Lucretia Mott was regarded as the moral force behind the movement. Until the Civil War, conventions similar to that in Seneca Falls were held almost every year. While that terrible conflict lasted, conventions were abandoned because the women were heavily involved in other activities such as nursing and relief. The National Woman's Loyal League was formed and ultimately collected 400,000 signatures to a petition asking Congress to pass the Thirteenth Amendment.

Feminist leaders had expected that the reward for women's war work would be the vote. That was not to be. First consideration would be given to Negro men. Division among the women followed. Dissent arose over the proposed wording of the Fourteenth Amendment. Anthony and Stanton contended that the word *male,* used for the first time in the Constitution, would make it more difficult for women to get the ballot. Susan Anthony, although a sincere abolitionist, declared, "I will cut off this right arm of mine before I will even work for or demand the ballot for the Negro and not woman." Stanton warned that male Negro suffrage caused "an antagonism between black men and all women that will culminate in fearful outrages on womanhood, especially in the southern states." These women believed that suffrage for blacks and women should and could be gained concurrently.

Many Republican politicians, as well as some feminists, were convinced that introducing the female vote would jeopardize suffrage for Negro males. This group included Frederick Douglass, Horace Greeley, Wendell Phillips, and other notables who had been sympathetic to women's rights. Despite great effort on the part of the Anthony-Stanton camp to secure petitions against the Fourteenth Amendment, it was ratified in 1868 with the proposed wording, which extended indirect suffrage provisions to black men, with no mention of women.

A second disappointment to the suffragist movement was the failure of the Fifteenth Amendment, passed two years later, to include the word *sex* where it was specified that suffrage could not be denied on account of race, color, or previous condition of servitude.

Shortly after the ratification of the Fourteenth Amendment, Senator Samuel Pomeroy of Kansas introduced in Congress the first constitutional amendment on woman suffrage. Many more introductions would be required before victory.

In 1869, differences led to the formation of two groups of feminists. The National Woman Suffrage Association, led by Anthony, was the more militant of the two and decided to exclude men. It was dedicated to obtaining the vote by a constitutional amendment; such amendments were sometimes called Anthony Amendments. The National also concerned itself with other issues such as improving the lot of women and children in the labor force, "fallen women," and divorce. The more conservative group called itself the American Woman Suffrage Association. Its strategy was a state-by-state approach to amend individual state constitutions, an approach more acceptable to Southern women. Led by Henry Ward Beecher, Lucy Stone, and Julia Ward Howe, it had less interest in unions, prostitution, and divorce. There was antagonism between Stone and Anthony, but how much this influenced the formation of two separate organizations is not known. The two organizations remained separated for 20 years.

The legislature of the territory of Wyoming passed a woman suffrage bill in 1869. Moreover, it provided that once on the voting lists, women were entitled to sit on juries.

Women were attempting to vote in various states. In 1875, a Missouri woman named Virginia Minor sued for the right to vote. The Supreme Court ruled that the Fourteenth Amendment had not created any new voters and therefore did not grant Minor the right to vote.

When Carrie became active in the suffrage movement, the prospect of success at an early date was not encouraging. At the same time, people's thinking was gradually changing, a hopeful sign for the suffragist.

Through the efforts of Alice Stone Blackwell, the National and the American Associations were reconciled. Blackwell was the daughter of Lucy Stone and Henry Blackwell, the latter as ardent a supporter of women's rights as his wife. A joint convention took place in Washington, D.C., in 1890, close to the time of Susan Anthony's 70th birthday. Carrie, then 31, attended as part of the Iowa delegation. She heard the 74-year-old Stanton make her presidential speech as leader of the new united organization, the National American Woman Suffrage Association (NAWSA). Other celebrities, now gray and well past their prime, were seen at the activities. Carrie addressed the gathering, donating her fee to campaign in South Dakota the coming November. She has been described as a gifted speaker, and this attribute no doubt contributed to her future success.

In June, Carrie was married in Seattle to George W. Catt, a structural engineer. They had known each other in Ames and had met again in San Francisco. An advocate of votes for women, Catt agreed that his wife would have ample time to devote to the cause of suffrage. Through Catt's connections with the Great Northern Railway, Carrie became aware of the boom in the Puget Sound area—an atmosphere different from that in the Midwest.

That summer, Carrie participated in a campaign in South Dakota. When the state had been admitted to the Union in 1889, it adopted Prohibition. The anti–Prohibition forces were marshaled to fight the referendum, for the great majority of women favored Prohibition. Carrie's area was the central plain, with the Missouri River its western border. A five-year drought had created a land of desolation. Her assigned stops were poverty-stricken remote area where only a handful of families lived.

For weeks she addressed meetings in schoolhouses, farmhouses, and grain elevators, being put up wherever a family receptive to woman suffrage offered shelter (Susan B. Anthony had been doing this type of thing for decades).

Dismayed by the campaign's lack of organization, Carrie wrote to South Dakota's suffrage headquarters, "With the exception of the work of a few women, nothing is being done. We have opposed to us the most powerful political elements in the state. Continuing as we are, we cannot poll 20,000 votes. We are converting women to 'want to vote' by the hundreds, but we are having no appreciable effect on the men." And of course it was the men who voted.

The results showed 22,000 votes for and 45,000 votes against. Carrie listed for future use the essentials of winning a referendum: (1) endorsement by great citizens' organizations, (2) endorsement by the political parties, (3) an adequate campaign fund. Never again would she be involved in a fruitless effort, bound to fail from lack of preparation alone.

One bright spot in 1890 was Wyoming's entry into the Union as the first state with a constitution providing for woman suffrage.

Two years later, the Catts were living in Brooklyn, New York, because of the expansion of George Catt's business. That summer, Carrie returned to her home state to organize a Mississippi Valley conference in Des Moines. Miss Anthony was sufficiently impressed with Carrie's efforts to make her finance chairman of the NAWSA.

Colorado followed Wyoming by granting the vote to women in 1893. Carrie had campaigned in the larger towns and mining centers and at most of the party conventions. The next year she participated in an unsuccessful campaign in Kansas. With travel facilities poor in sparsely settled areas of the state, it was often difficult for her to meet her commitments. Despite this, she managed to speak in all but two of the state's 105 counties.

A banner year for the cause was 1896 when Utah and Idaho were added to the victory column.

Because of her campaign activities and a successful tour of some

Southern states, Carrie was made chairman of the Organization Committee and given instructions to draw up a plan for the coming year. In doing this, she focused on 10 states that appeared to lack any organization where there were few known supporters. She also compiled a much needed directory of the clubs and their officers, finding that the club total was 800. During 1889, Carrie's last year in that office, she spent 64 days and 28 nights on trains that covered more than 13,000 miles.

The day came when age forced Susan B. Anthony, still regarded the suffrage movement's great leader, to step down as president of the NAWSA. A likely successor was her coworker and closest friend, Anna Howard Shaw. Dr. Shaw, a minister and physician, had worked long and hard in the association and was known as a gifted orator. It was no secret that she greatly desired the position. On the other hand, Alice Blackwell decided to promote Carrie (Alice's mother had died, but it was known that she was impressed with Carrie). Despite her regard for Dr. Shaw, Anthony's choice was the younger woman. Although Carrie would receive no pay as president, George Catt encouraged his wife to stand for the office. She was elected in February 1900.

When introduced by the retiring president, the new president said:

> Since Miss Anthony announced her intention to retire, there have been editorials in many leading papers, expressing approval of her but not of the cause. She has been much larger than our association. The papers have spoken of the new president as Miss Anthony's successor. Miss Anthony never will have a successor. A president chosen from the younger workers is on a level with the association.... The cause has got beyond where one woman can do the whole. I shall not be its leader as Miss Anthony has been; I can only be an officer of this association. I will do all I can, but I cannot do it without the cooperation of all of you.

Carrie served in the position until 1904. She was well aware of the opposition: liquor interests feared that women would vote "dry"; business interests assumed that female voters would press for labor and social reforms; the South resisted the enfranchisement of black women and intended to continue having states establish their own voting qualifications, a situation that would be threatened by a federal amendment. It was not only men that needed to be enlightened; many women still saw no need for enfranchisement. No more states were gained during the Catt presidency; in fact, there were no such victories until 1910 when the state of Washington by a 2–1 vote permitted women to vote.

A bazaar reminiscent of those so successful for antislavery societies was held during the first year of Carrie's tenure. The site was Madison Square Garden, and state suffrage associations sponsored booths where their products were sold—pralines and pecans from Louisiana, citrus fruits from Florida, a carload of flour and 200 pounds of butter from Kansas turned into freshly baked bread to be eaten on the spot, and so on. Mrs. McKinley and Mrs. Roosevelt, wives of the president and vice president, respectively, contributed dolls, as did a Sioux woman. Even an automobile, costing all of $700, was made available for Carrie to transport honored guests. The affair netted $10,000 and gave the cause excellent publicity.

After four years, Carrie announced that she would not stand for reelection but had no intention of retiring from suffrage work. Apparently she needed a rest. The experience gained in the presidency served as a prelude to a later highly productive term in the office.

When asked to direct a campaign in Oregon in the fall of 1905, Carrie had declined, writing, "All I have done for the suffrage cause during the last fifteen years, I have been enabled to do by my husband's generosity.... I should dearly love to undertake the work in Oregon, but my husband needs me now, and is going to need me more and more, and I will not leave him." George Catt died soon afterward at the age of 45, willing his wife a considerable fortune.

After her husband's death, Carrie took into her home Mary Garrett Hay, a suffragist from Indiana with whom she had worked closely and would continue until Miss Hay's death in 1928.

For 10 years Carrie's energy was spent in building up the International Woman Suffrage Alliance, expanding its membership from 8 to 25 branches. In the course of this work, she traveled extensively in Europe.

In 1910, Carrie was at a sanitarium in Dansville, New York, recuperating from an illness. When urged to take a rest, she decided on a world tour on behalf of woman suffrage. It occupied parts of the years 1910 and 1911 and brought her into contact with numerous notables. She was in South Africa when the welcome news arrived that a special election in California had given its women the right to vote (Oregon would follow in 1912).

Carrie resigned from the presidency of the International Alliance to lead a crucial campaign in New York state, the election there scheduled for November 1915. Despite very thorough coverage, the New York campaign failed, as had so many others. But it polled 42 percent of the vote. According to the *New York World*, this was "a revelation of the astonishing growth of the movement."

In 1915, Carrie was again elected president of the NAWSA, replacing Dr. Shaw, who had led it since 1904. Seven of the 48 states were in the yes column—not a cheering prospect considering the time and effort expended. On the encouraging side, Mrs. Frank Leslie, widow of the publisher of *Leslie's Weekly*, left the bulk of her estate to Carrie to apply "as she shall think most advisable to the furtherance of the cause of woman suffrage, to which she has so worthily devoted so many years of her life."

Litigation followed, but Carrie eventually received more than $900,000, which went to the suffrage cause.

Some suffragists, impatient with the long and seemingly nonproductive struggle, were turning to another leader. Alice Paul had studied in England and was familiar with the tactics of the British suffragettes; she had been imprisoned for militant activity. Backing up her leadership was Lucy Burns, who also had studied abroad and had been an organizer of the Edinburgh Women's Social and Political Union. These two women established the Congressional Union (which later became the Women's Party) and gave up affiliation with the NAWSA. Their group favored the Anthony Amendment. When the latter was brought before Congress in 1914–1915, the Senate voted 35–34 against it; the House, 204–174. (The Constitution states that two-thirds of both houses must propose an amendment and that the amendment must be ratified by three-fourths of the state legislatures.) Paul's group focused public attention on women's rights by parades and picketing in addition to the more usual methods of the day. It deserves much credit for refocusing attention on the Anthony Amendment.

Probably influenced by the still-recent experience in New York state, Carrie too decided that the time had come for the NAWSA to make a more concentrated push for the federal amendment and simultaneously to pressure for state referenda. Her plan was adopted at an emergency meeting held at Atlantic City in 1916. Here is part of it:

> We should win, if it is possible to do so, a few more states before the Federal Amendment gets up to the legislatures.... A southern state should be selected and made ready for a campaign, and the solid front of the "anti" South broken as soon as possible.
>
> Some break in the solid "anti" East should be made too. If New York wins in 1917, the backbone of the opposition will be largely bent if not broken....
>
> By 1920, when the next national party platforms will be adopted, we should have won Iowa, South Dakota, North Dakota, Nebraska, New York, Maine and a southern state. We should have secured the Illinois law [presidential suffrage by act of the legislature, granted by Illinois in 1913] in a number of other states.
>
> With these victories to our credit and the tremendous increase of momentum given the whole movement, we should be able to secure planks in all platforms favoring the Federal amendment (if it has not passed before that time) and to secure its passage in the December term of the 1920 Congress.
>
> It should then go the legislatures of thirty-nine states which meet in 1921, and the remaining states would have the opportunity to ratify the amendment in 1922. If thirty-six states had ratified in these two years, the end of our struggle would come by April 1, 1922, six years hence.

The officers of 36 state suffrage associations signed to carry out the plan, but the details were to be kept secret so that "neither the enemy nor friends will discover where the real battle is—[for the federal amendment]." As we shall see, Carrie overestimated the time required.

In 1917, New York granted woman suffrage. In the same year, North Dakota, Ohio, Indiana, Rhode Island, and Michigan voted to follow the Illinois law. Unfortunately, the Indiana and Ohio laws were soon rescinded.

Following the entry of the United States into World War I on April 6, 1917, women poured into the work force in large numbers. They also served as volunteers in various capacities—working for the Red Cross, selling Liberty bonds, and so on. Carrie insisted that *both* the war effort and suffrage must be served. The women's contribution was outstanding and undoubtedly hastened the day so long awaited by millions of women.

In January 1918, President Wilson committed himself to woman suffrage. The House passed the Anthony Amendment, but the Senate defeated it. In 1919, there was sufficient support for the Anthony Amendment that some 24 state legislatures petitioned Congress to submit a federal woman suffrage amendment for state ratification. In May of that year, the 66th Congress was called by the president to a special session. The House passed the Anthony Amendment 304–89. Senate approval followed in June. On August 26, 1920, when Tennessee became the 36th state to ratify, the Nineteenth Amendment became the law of the land, at long last making women eligible to vote.

Even before ratification was accomplished, Carrie had presented to the NAWSA the idea for what would become the League of Women Voters. She envisioned a nonpartisan political organization that would educate women on how to exercise their new political rights. She also wanted this league to address political corruption and to work for child-labor reform and protective legislation for employed women. The League of Women Voters (LWV) was founded in 1920. Its first president was Maud Wood Peck, who had worked closely with Carrie and would later write her biography. Carrie became honorary chairman, holding the position until she died.

After the vote was won, Carrie continued her international suffrage work. Another interest was the peace movement. She was a strong supporter of the League of Nations and later of the United Nations. With Nettie R. Shuler she authored *Woman Suffrage and Politics: The Inner Story of the Suffrage Movement,* and with others she contributed to *Why Wars Must Cease.*

Carrie received honorary degrees from four American institutions. Her international efforts were not forgotten; the women of the Philippines gave her a silver plaque to commemorate her assistance to them in their struggle for political rights; a 1935 Turkish postage stamp was struck in her honor; Finland bestowed its White Rose.

Carrie Chapman Catt (no date). Courtesy of Library of Congress.

Carrie Chapman Catt died in 1947 in New Rochelle, New York, where she had purchased a home in 1928.

When a three-cent stamp was designed in honor of the 100th anniversary of Seneca Falls, Carrie's portrait was placed between those of Lucretia Mott and Elizabeth Stanton.

Much has been written about the women who led the suffragist movement in this country. In general they were reformers. In the early days they were concerned with antislavery and temperance activities. Later they worked for peace and labor legislation that would benefit women and children. The majority were native white women, well educated and middle class. Most of them were guilty of nativism, although Jane Addams, who served as NAWSA's vice president from 1911 to 1913, was a noted exception; some agreed with Stanton that the electorate should be educated.

Although Carrie was representative of the suffragist group, certain characteristics distinguished her. Pragmatism was one. She was no atheist, but there is little evidence that religion played a central role in her life; however, she realized that it was important to the majority of Americans who voted. Elizabeth Cady Stanton, who believed that the Biblical concept of women as inferior to men impeded feminist progress, coauthored

Woman's Bible (1895–1898), which interpreted the Scriptures in ways that some people found distasteful. What Carrie really thought of the work is not clear. She once made a note that "the four great religious systems of the world command obedience and subjection [of women]," but she felt that the continuing criticism was hurting her cause and therefore voted to have the NAWSA disassociate itself from Stanton on the issue. Anthony, on the other hand, thought NAWSA owed Stanton loyalty, even though she did not approve of her colleague's writing. Carrie's nonpartisan attitude was another example of her pragmatism. Related to this was her failure to encourage picketing, an activity promoted by the Women's Party, because she knew that most male voters did not approve of it. Rather than alienate males, Carrie sought to gain and publicize the support of important men such as the president, so that the suffrage movement would represent a demand by progressive people—male and female. In other words, she found it practical to devote her energy to one issue—if necessary, at the expense of others.

As a Progressive, Carrie was also an optimist, believing in the evolution of the race and that progress was bound to come as the intelligent educated the ignorant. Above all, she had a genius for organization—a gift that was available at a time when thinking had become advanced enough to accept a woman's right to vote.

Today's Carrie's LWV encourages the informed and active participation of citizens in government and influences public policy through education and advocacy. It is organized to parallel the three levels of government: local, state, and national. Membership is open to women and men and numbers approximately 107,000. The national office of the League of Women Voters of the United States, located in Washington, D.C., houses a staff of approximately 45 and shares spaces with its sister organization, the League of Women Voters Education Fund. Programs and priorities have changed over the years, but the League has remained true to its historic mission of education and advocacy: (1) To expand citizen participation in the election process in federal, state, and local government decision making. (2) To secure public policies that promote League positions on member participation and agreement. The League arrives at its positions on issues through research, study, and consensus. Since its inception, it has remained nonpartisan, neither supporting nor opposing political parties or candidates for public office. On selected issues, the League does take an advocacy position.

In 1972, an equal rights amendment (ERA) was introduced. It was approved by Congress but failed to be ratified by three-quarters of the states. Would Carrie have supported it? She did not support the ERA introduced in 1923 because she believed in protective legislation for working women. Because she was progressive, her stand today might be different.

The right to abortion, child care, and pay equity are current burning feminist issues. Carrie was silent on the first. Although she was more concerned about women who had to work than those who wanted to work, she would probably vote for the provision of child care. As for pay equity, we can only guess. Whether any one of these as a single issue would influence her vote for president and other officials cannot be known. It is clear that she was aware of the responsibility granted to women by the Nineteenth Amendment. "Winning the vote is only an opening wedge," she declared. "To learn how to use it is a bigger task."

Margaret Mitchell

When the American Library Association in 1987 polled thousands about their favorite "best book read," the first choice by a wide margin was *Gone with the Wind.* It had been written more than half a century earlier by Margaret Mitchell, the subject of this chapter.

Her father was Eugene Mitchell, a lawyer who specialized in drawing wills and examining land titles. A somewhat inflexible man of great integrity, he was also an expert on Georgia history. Her mother was Maybelle (Stephens) Mitchell, a woman of Irish descent who remained a Roman Catholic. She read widely and was a dedicated suffragist—just the type of person Carrie Catt liked to have working for her in the South. The couple had three children: Stephens, who would become a lawyer and inherit the rights to his sister's masterpiece, and Margaret Munnerlyn, destined to become a world-famous author; another son died in infancy.

Margaret was born in Atlanta, Georgia, on November 9, 1900. At the turn of the century, Atlanta was growing, but a far cry from what it is today, having a population of about 90,000. Unlike the other women in this book, Margaret lived and died in one city and was associated with that city her entire life. According to Stephens, "Ours was one of the families that could refer to parents, grandparents and great-grandparents who had lived in or near [Atlanta]."

As a very young child, Margaret often rode her pony with aging veterans of the Lost Cause. From them she absorbed all sorts of details about the conflict. Both her grandfathers had fought for the Confederacy, so she had heard about it constantly at home. As with Juliette Low's Savannah, Atlanta still had bitter memories of General Sherman and the Union army. The effect of all this was expressed later as part of a radio interview. She said: "I heard about the fighting and the wounds and the primitive way they were treated—how ladies nursed in hospitals—the way gangrene smelled—what substitutes were used for food and clothing when the blockade got too tight for those necessities to be brought in from abroad. I heard about the burning and looting of Atlanta and the way the refugees crowded the roads and trains to Macon."

Margaret was educated in Atlanta public schools and at Washington

Seminary, a private school for girls. She graduated in 1918. By 1917, the United States had entered World War I, and some young ladies of Margaret's age were entertaining officers stationed at nearby military installations. Eventually Margaret became engaged to one of these young men, Clifford Henry, who shared her passion for dancing. He departed for France in 1918. According to various descriptions, Margaret at this time was of diminutive stature and had blue eyes and reddish-brown hair. Friends remarked on her sense of humor and considered her a good conversationalist.

She apparently hoped to become a psychiatrist and began by gaining admission to Smith College in the fall of 1918. It was not a good year. In October her fiancé was killed at St. Mihiel, earning the Croix de Guerre. Four months later, her mother died of influenza. Smith College was noted for its high academic standards, but Margaret managed to survive the freshman year. However, she did not return to complete the remaining three years, thus ending her plans for a medical career.

Eugene Mitchell appeared to be devastated by Maybelle's death. "It took weeks for him to recover from his first grief," Stephens remembered. Mitchell expected his daughter to manage the household. As his real-estate contracts suffered because of damage done by the boll weevil, money became scarce. In spite of that, the domestic staff consisted of four blacks—Bessie, the cook; Cammie, only 15; a man who did the yardwork; and a laundress who came in twice a week. Margaret's grandmother, Annie Stephens, and a younger unmarried sister, moved in. Quite understandably, there was often friction between the younger woman and her elderly relatives.

To add to Margaret's troubles, Eugene Mitchell became more and more perverse. He did arrange for Margaret's membership in the Debutante Club. Her acceptance led him to assume that she would be asked to join Atlanta's Junior League. It was the flapper era, and from all accounts, Margaret entered into the life with gusto, rebelling at prevailing customs and at odds with the older generation. A flirt, she smoked in public, was known as a drinker (although Prohibition was the law of the land), and appears to have been a show-off. Such conduct apparently did not make a good impression on those in control of Atlanta's high society, for she was not invited to join the Junior League, a snub she did not forget for some time.

Margaret had retained her love of riding. In February 1920, she sustained serious damage to one leg when she tried to jump a horse over a stone wall. A previous injury exacerbated the condition, and she was laid up for several months. To her chagrin, she was ordered to wear corrective shoes. (She once wrote to a friend, "I have to wear high-laced shoes on account of my ankle, and no matter what I wear I look awful.") This was one of several accidents that befell Margaret Mitchell.

The period of the early twenties was not one in which Georgia and Atlanta could take pride. During Reconstruction, the Ku Klux Klan had tried to restore white supremacy by various means. The organization was first revived in Georgia in 1915 and by 1925 boasted as many as 5 million members nationwide. With headquarters in Atlanta, its influence spread quickly throughout the South and to parts of the Midwest, Southwest, and the Far West. Klansmen were responsible for beatings, kidnappings, arson, and murder. Still dedicated to white supremacy, they worked to put into political positions persons receptive to their philosophy. Blacks in Atlanta, as elsewhere, lived in terror of this menace. Cammie, for example, was afraid to be in the vicinity of the headquarters and refused to leave the Mitchell house after dark. Margaret had a paternalistic attitude toward blacks. Her thinking was far from emancipated, but she felt affection for them, not hostility or hate. Bessie worked for Margaret for many years, and it is clear that Margaret felt responsible for her in the social sense.

With life rather unexciting for her, it is not surprising that Margaret turned to one of her many admirers. He was Berrien Kinnard Upshaw, known as Red, the handsome son of a respectable old Georgia family. They had met at a dance when he was a University of Georgia football player (he had entered the Naval Academy but dropped out). Some considered him emotionally unstable, but Margaret did not seem to notice this. He was a fast driver, a heavy drinker—pugnacious and generally reckless. There was a suspicion that he earned his living bootlegging. Nevertheless, Margaret seemed to be attracted to him. They were married on September 2, 1922, over the objection of Eugene Mitchell. The bride had left the Catholic church of her mother; the groom professed no religion, so the ceremony was performed at the Mitchell residence.

The couple moved into Margaret's family home. Disagreements developed, and Upshaw wanted to be under another roof. Peggy refused to leave until he had better prospects of employment. Her husband began to get drunk and abusive, and in a few months he and Margaret separated, planning on a divorce.

With her husband out of the picture, Margaret was often seen with John Marsh, Upshaw's friend and best man, a Kentuckian who had served overseas in the war. He had taught English, worked on the staff of three newspapers, and was a copy editor for the Associated Press in Atlanta. He left newspaper work in 1924 for a public-relations position at Georgia Power and Light. John was very different from Upshaw, neither glamorous nor daring, but dependable and steadfast. Margaret at first seemed to need him as a friend; by 1925, they were engaged.

With no support from Upshaw, Margaret needed work. In December 1922, she obtained a job as a cub reporter for the *Atlanta Journal* magazine at $25 a week. The byline for her first assignment was Margaret Mitchell

Upshaw. For the next, she requested Peggy Mitchell, using that for the four years she was with the *Journal* (when she was young, she seems to have preferred Peggy to Margaret). A desk and chair were procured for her, but the legs required sawing down to accommodate her stature.

William Howland of the *Journal* described its headquarters as an "old five-story, smoke-stained, rat-infested, roach-ridden red brick building which rose in grimy ruggedness above the railroad tracks. . . . Perhaps most rugged of all was the third floor back office in which the *Sunday Magazine* was quartered." Margaret named this single room with its soot-covered windows the Black Hole of Calcutta.

On the job long hours every day for six days a week, her pieces were on diverse subjects: Rudolph Valentino, the Italian star of a silent movie, *The Sheik;* Calvin Coolidge, the vice president; bootleggers; politicians; camp meetings; questions of the day. Sometimes she arranged for stunt photography to accompany the text. Medora Field Perkerson, the magazine's assistant editor and later the author of popular mysteries, believed that Margaret's articles "mirrored the flapper era. . . . [She] recorded the changing skirt lengths . . . the earliest boyish bobs, the strange slang of the 'Flaming Youth' period as reflected in Atlanta." Margaret wrote 139 by-lined features and 85 news stories. She filled in here and there, even composing a chapter for the weekly serial when the manuscript was lost. Curiously, she wrote her ending first, her beginning last. John Marsh often gave editorial assistance. She sometimes interviewed older citizens. "I was interested in how people felt during the siege of Atlanta," she once said, noting that many of her questions had nothing to do with the story at hand. She "just wanted to know these things."

Margaret was one among several of the *Journal's* staff who later became known in literary circles. She and Erskine Caldwell were the most famous. Among other works, Caldwell wrote *Tobacco Road.* For a few years he was married to Margaret Bourke-White, whom we shall meet in the next chapter. Margaret Mitchell's stint with the *Atlanta Journal* certainly sharpened her writing skills. Her success there improved her self-image, and in all, she could look back on the experience as a happy and satisfying one.

In October 1924, she was granted an uncontested divorce on the grounds of cruel treatment (even after the separation, Upshaw returned and beat her severely). She married John Marsh on July 4, 1925, at the Unitarian-Universalist Church. The Marshes moved into a small apartment they named the Dump. They hired a part-time cook-housekeeper, and when they entertained, most of their friends were newspaper people.

Towards the end of 1925, Margaret was assigned a two-piece feature about the five Confederate generals to be cut in granite for the Stone Mountain Memorial. With little time until deadline for the first, she went to the Carnegie Library to read. The editor was so impressed with the first article that he decided to run four instead of two pieces and permitted an increase in length.

Margaret quit her job in May 1926. John had received a raise, and she agreed to stay at home. She would, however, freelance for a weekly *Journal* column called "Elizabeth Bennet's Gossip." She gave this up after a short time.

That fall she had an auto accident that resulted in a third injury to her ankle. Being laid up for weeks made her depressed. (We note here that from this time until the end of her life, Margaret seemed to suffer some sort of illness much of the time.) Early in 1927 she was at least able to use crutches.

Around that time she decided to begin the historical novel she had in mind—the work that John had been pressing her to write. The background was naturally what she had heard and read about Atlanta in the antebellum period, the Civil War, and Reconstruction. With her Remington portable typewriter on top of a sewing table, she began, as usual, at the end of her story. As time went by, a pile of manila envelopes accumulated near the typewriter. When acquaintances visited, she removed the green eyeshade she wore while she typed and placed a large towel over the work area. Close friends knew that she was writing a book that required research at the Carnegie Library, but that was about all they knew.

As John read the manuscript, he made editorial corrections and sometimes comments. No writer himself, he seems to have been a good critic. Above all, he encouraged his wife because he was genuinely enthusiastic about the project.

In 1928, the part-time domestic was replaced by the Mitchells' Bessie, who came to work full-time and would remain a faithful friend. Margaret now had ample time for writing the novel. She worked hard, sometimes making several revisions of a part with which she was dissatisfied. By the spring of 1929, there were 20 manila envelopes containing hundreds of thousands of words. The first chapter was unsatisfactory, and there were other unresolved problems. She did little to solve them for about a year. She was suffering from arthritis and not inclined to concentrate. John recognized his wife's talent as something he would have "given the world to possess" and was disturbed that she would not complete the work.

One friend especially interested in the manuscript was Lois Cole, who represented Macmillan Publishing Company in Atlanta. She knew little about the story but correctly judged Margaret's capabilities. Cole returned to New York in 1932 to work in the home office. In December 1933, as assistant editor, she wrote a formal letter to Margaret stating that Macmillan would like to see the novel, either finished or as it was. Margaret replied that she had not completed the book, that she doubted she ever would or that it would be worth seeing. However, she promised to submit it first to Macmillan if she did finish it.

In 1934, Margaret had another automobile accident, which injured her spine, necessitating a brace for months. This provided an excuse for delaying work on the book. Otherwise, things were going well. John had advanced in the utility company, and the Marshes had moved to a larger apartment.

In April 1935, Harold Latham, Macmillan's vice president and editor in chief, was in Atlanta, touring the South in search of manuscripts for publication. Thanks to Lois Cole, he knew of the work in progress at the Marsh apartment. When he asked Margaret why she had not submitted it to a publisher, she told him she didn't think the book would sell because the heroine was in love with another woman's husband for years and they never did anything about it. When Latham asked if he could see it, she at first refused. To his surprise, she changed her mind, coming to his hotel with her large stack of manila envelopes. On the train to New Orleans Latham started to read. Despite the fact that the manuscript still needed considerable work, he knew that he had found treasure in Atlanta.

For the 25th anniversary of the publication of *Gone with the Wind*, Lois Cole wrote about her first real contact with the novel:

> The manuscript arrived, and I spent evenings reading it, breaking off late and reluctantly. It was, physically, one of the worst manuscripts I have ever seen. There was no first chapter (Peggy had tried six or seven and liked none), but Chapter Two was neatly typed on white paper. So was Chapter Three. Then came pages and pages of yellow paper, written over in pencil, and often three or four versions of one scene. Then came more final chapters, then some would be missing entirely. There were two entirely different accounts of Frank's death. The last chapter was in final form. . . . In spite of all the difficulties of reading the manuscript, I knew it was one of the most fascinating novels of all time.

Margaret must have regretted her impulsive and irresponsible act—she had given up her only copy, poor as it was from the standpoint of appearances—for she wired Latham in New Orleans to return it. He wrote her that what he had read impressed him and that he wanted to finish it.

In addition to Lois Cole, Macmillan consulted Professor Charles Everett of Columbia University's Department of English about the unusual manuscript. "This is the story of the formation of a woman's character," he wrote in part of his reply, "in the peace and quiet of plantation life before the war, in the crisis of the Civil War, and in the privation of the reconstruction period. . . . By all means take the book. It can't possibly turn out badly. . . . Tell the author not to do anything to it but bridge the few obvious gaps and strengthen the last page."

The outcome was that in July Margaret received a contract with an advance of $500. Having a definite deadline put her to work. She was determined that every historical detail—the weather at a specific time, the price of cotton on a certain day, and so forth—should be correct, and she checked them again laboriously.

The title had to be selected. Professor Everett had suggested *Another Day*, but Margaret thought of others, including *Not in Our Stars*. By the end of October, she had submitted *Gone with the Wind*, taken from the third stanza of Ernest Dowson's poem, *"Non sum qualis Eram Bonae sub regno Cynara"*:

> Last night, ah, yesternight, betwixt her lips and mine
> There fell thy shadow, Cynara! thy breath was shed
> Upon my soul between the kisses and the wine;
> And I was desolate and sick of an old passion,
> Yea, I was desolate and bowed my head:
> I have been faithful to thee, Cynara! in my fashion.

> All night upon mine heart I felt her warm heart beat,
> Night-long within mine arms in love and sleep she lay;
> Surely the kisses of her bought red mouth were sweet;
> But I was desolate and sick of an old passion,
> When I awoke and found the dawn was gray:
> I have been faithful to thee, Cynara! in my fashion.

> I have forgot much, Cynara! gone with the wind,
> Flung roses, roses riotously with the throng,
> Dancing, to put thy pale, lost lilies out of mind;
> But I was desolate and sick of an old passion,
> Yea, all the time, because the dance was long:
> I have been faithful to thee, Cynara! in my fashion.

> I cried for madder music and for stronger wine,
> But when the feast is finished and the lamps expire,
> Then falls thy shadow, Cynara! the night is thine;
> And I am desolate and sick of an old passion,
> Yea hungry for the lips of my desire:
> I have been faithful to thee, Cynara! in my fashion.

She noted that there was no relation in thought and idea between her book and the poem. William Lyon Phelps has pointed out that it is likely that Dowson got the phrase from a similar passage in a poem by the famous Irish poet James Clarence Mangan (1803–1849).

As for the professor's comment about the ending, Margaret wrote Latham, "I think she [Scarlett] got him [Rhett] in the end." But her intention was "to leave the end open to the reader." And she left it that way. She also prided herself on her presentation of the Negro dialect and had John write that she did not want changes made by editors (she had to make some compromises on this).

Margaret Mitchell about 1936. Courtesy of Sophia Smith Collection, Smith College.

With the help of a typist supplied by Macmillan and John's secretary from the power company, the final draft—well over 400,000 words with revisions, deletions, bridges, and so on—was on its way some six months after issuance of the contract. The publication date was set for June 30. The author dedicated her book to John, but she used her maiden name on the title page. She was then 35.

Macmillan spent a large sum on its prepublication advertising. This paid off. The Book-of-the-Month Club ordered 50,000 copies, and David O. Selznick's studio offered $50,000 for the movie rights.

A best-seller from the first day of publication, *Gone with the Wind* remained on the list for 21 consecutive months. By then, 2 million copies had been sold in the United States and 1 million abroad. Worldwide, the book continues to sell more than 100,000 copies a year. In this country, more than 200,000 paperback copies are sold annually.

As we have seen, Margaret acted in an ambivalent way about submitting her manuscript. Her reaction to fame was enigmatic. She resented the public's invasion of her privacy, complaining, for example, about the huge number of phone calls from strangers. Yet she did not have an unlisted phone number until near the time of her death. John continued to work for Georgia Power, but he also handled all *Gone with the Wind* rights to foreign translations, a chore that occupied much of his free time. Fan letters were voluminous, and Margaret answered almost every one, often with long letters that brought replies, which she sometimes answered. Since these letters, along with those she wrote to reviewers, give better insight into her novel, they have been of great value to scholars. Perhaps writing them let her rationalize that she had no opportunity to write another novel. (She also refused all offers for articles.) The fact remains that although *Gone with the Wind* left the Marshes wealthy enough to do as they pleased, they led rather harassed lives, plagued with ill health.

One never-to-be-forgotten event in Margaret's life was the premiere of the movie. Scheduled for December 15, 1939, it was a major event for Atlanta—indeed for all Georgia since the governor had declared the 15th a state holiday. Various festivities took place, including a parade and a charity ball sponsored by the Junior League held the previous evening at the Atlanta Municipal Auditorium. Margaret was conspicuous by her absence at the latter event. Half of the city's 300,000 people turned out to greet the motorcade that carried visitors from the airport, among them Vivien Leigh, Clark Gable, and Olivia De Havilland (Leslie Howard had returned to serve his native England, then at war; Hattie McDaniel and the other black members of the cast did not come to segregated Atlanta). David Selznick, Harold Latham, and Lois Cole came, as well as the governors of Florida, Alabama, Georgia, South Carolina, and Tennessee. Where possible, Atlanta was dressed in the architecture of the 1860s, and its citizens dressed accordingly. Loew's Grand Theatre, the scene of the premiere, had a false front to simulate Tara. The capacity was just over 2,000, so seats were at a premium. Four aged veterans who had fought in the battle of Atlanta had been invited and were wearing Confederate uniforms.

Margaret, attired in pale pink, entered the theatre just after Clark Gable. The master of ceremonies inquired, "Aren't you proud of your wife, John?" John Marsh's reply was heard over the loudspeaker: "I was proud of her even before she wrote a book." Margaret was led to a seat beside John Hay Whitney, the financier behind Selznick International.

At the close of the spectacular film, so faithful to Margaret's masterpiece and distinguished by its fine acting and magnificent musical score,

Margaret Mitchell with Vivien Leigh, Clark Gable, and David Selznick, Atlanta 1939. Courtesy of Sophia Smith Collection, Smith College.

Atlanta's mayor called for the stars and the producer, then asked Gable to escort Margaret to the stage. She graciously offered profuse thanks to the many who had contributed to the success of the evening. She continued, "But I just want to speak for one moment about Mr. David Selznick. He's the man that every one of you cracked that joke, 'Oh, well, we'll wait till Shirley Temple grows up and *she'll* play Scarlett.' I want to commend Mr. Selznick's courage and his obstinacy and his determination in just keeping his mouth shut until he got exactly the cast he wanted, in spite of everything everybody said. And I think you're going to agree with me—that he had the absolutely perfect cast." (It was reported that at the close of the movie, Selznick was found in the hallway, tears in his eyes.) The applause for Margaret was overwhelming. The night indeed belonged to Margaret Mitchell, just as Clark Gable had said it should.

The Pulitzer Prize and the American Booksellers' Association award went to Margaret in 1937. Smith College bestowed an honorary degree on her, and a one-cent stamp was issued in her honor in 1986. There was a 1990 commemorative stamp for the movie.

Margaret's death came in 1949 as the result of an automobile accident. John died three years later. They left no children.

It is assumed that the reader is familiar with *Gone with the Wind.* If not, start it, and become hooked on it, as have millions of others before you.

There has been much speculation about the characters. Margaret stated that the young black girl Prissy was based on Cammie, the 15-year-old that worked in the Mitchell household when Margaret took over its management. She admitted only that resemblance. There are other striking similarities: Ashley Wilkes and Margaret's dead fiancé, Rhett Butler and her first husband, Scarlett and Margaret herself, to name a few. This is not surprising, since an author reflects her life experiences. Comparisons have also been made between Margaret's characters and various characters in classical literature, the most frequent being that of Scarlett and Becky Sharp. However, Margaret claimed that she had not read *Vanity Fair* before her book went to press. She said she wrote of "some people who went up and some who went down, those who take it and those who couldn't."

In a 1975 review, James Michener noted that "the elemental fact about this novel is its extraordinary readability." This is exactly what Margaret aimed for: "simplicity of ideas, of construction, of words." She wrote a friend: "Despite its length and many details it is basically just a simple yarn of fairly simple people. There's no fine writing, there's no philosophizing, there is a minimum of description, there are no grandiose thoughts, there are no hidden meanings, no symbolism, nothing sensational—nothing, nothing at all that made other best sellers best sellers."

Reviewers like Kenneth Fowler have realized the power of her style:

> A few of the commentators on *Gone with the Wind* have mentioned the style as "undistinguished." We should like to say to that if, to provide a book as absorbing and exciting as this, it is necessary to give it an "undistinguished style," we are all for more of this kind of style in American letters. As a matter of fact, Miss Mitchell's style is deceptive—so simple and smooth-flowing that, lulled by its very perfection, one may easily overlook many passages of exceptional merit.

A frequent complaint is the narrow focus on Atlanta. The answer to that is that Margaret wrote about the locale she knew. Some academics have expressed scorn for the book. Here is a comment of Bernard De Voto made in 1937:

> *Gone with the Wind* is important as a phenomenon but hardly as a novel. It has too little thought and no philosophical overtones. It documents very well the daily life of a society at war and under reconstruction, but its ideas are rudimentary. Its author has no eye and no feeling of human character, and its page by page reliance on all formulas of sentimental

romance and all the effects of melodrama is offensive. The size of its public is significant; the book is not.

More serious is the criticism that centers around race relationships. In 1936, Malcolm Cowley complained that "*Gone with the Wind* is an encyclopedia of the plantation legend," showing "the band of faithful retainers, including two that quaintly resemble Aunt Jemima and Old Black Joe, ... the knightliness of the Ku Klux Klansmen, who frighten Negroes away from the polls, thus making Georgia safe for democracy and virtuous womanhood...." In 1975, Michener criticized the book's "highly restricted view of Negro liberation." Perhaps representative of the viewpoint of many blacks is an open letter to David Selznick. It was written by Carleton Moss in the *Daily Worker* January 9, 1940. Excerpts of that letter:

> If for nothing else but its distortion of the reconstruction period, GWTW ranks as a reactionary film and there is plenty else. For years, this deliberate falsification of a progressive era in American life has been fed the American schoolboy and to the American people through the stage and screen. The most repeated lies about the Civil War and the Reconstruction period are:
> 1. That the Negro didn't care about or want his freedom.
> 2. That he had neither the qualities nor the "innate" ability to take care of, let alone govern, himself.
>
> • • • •
>
> I have already alluded to the lopsided treatment of the Negro people in the mass scenes. Then there's that Bourbon belly-chuckle, the scene with the Negro chasing the chicken and numerous little scenes with the Negro slaves hopping up supplying "master's" wants before they are even asked for.
> As to the principal Negro characters, they follow the time-worn stereotype pattern laid down by Hollywood. There is shiftless and dull-witted Pork, young Prissie, indolent and thoroughly irresponsible, "Big" Sam with his radiant acceptance of slavery and Mammy with her constant haranguing and doting on every wish of Scarlett. It is made to appear that she loves this degrading position in the service of a family that has helped to keep her people enchained for centuries. This false collection of two-dimensioned Negro characters is insulting to the Negro people. Especially is this so since history provides us with such positive Negro characters as Nat Turner, Denmark Vesey, Gabriel Prosser, Fred Douglass, Harriet Tubman, Sojourner Truth, etc., and thousands of others who participated in the operation of the Underground Railroad, unflinchingly sacrificing their lives for the eventual freedom of their people and the ultimate completion of American democracy.

The only response to this is that *Gone with the Wind* was written exclusively from the contemporary Confederate viewpoint.

Despite the critics and the academics, *Gone with the Wind* remains a page-turner that has provided and continues to provide countless hours of enjoyable reading to millions. Scarlett and Rhett and "Tomorrow is another day" are part of our culture. Margaret's enduring monument remains, as Michener has said, "a titanic tale of human passions, loved around the world."

A 1991 book is *Scarlet: The Sequel to Margaret Mitchell's "Gone with the Wind."* Warren Books obtained the rights from Margaret's estate and then chose Alexandra Ripley as the author.

Margaret Bourke-White

Margaret Bourke-White wrote of her "insatiable desire to be on the spot when history is being made." In fulfilling that desire, she accumulated experiences granted to few persons, male or female, and gave the world the extraordinary photographs that remain her enduring monument.

Born in New York City on June 14, 1904, she was the second child of Joseph and Minnie (Bourke) White, who gave her a Jewish-Irish heritage. The family soon moved to Bound Brook, New Jersey, where Margaret grew up in a loving atmosphere. Mr. White was an engineer who designed printing equipment. Mrs. Bourke set high standards for her daughter, expecting her to have lofty aims. Although her father was a camera buff, Margaret showed no particular interest in photography. It was insects that commanded her attention at first (as an accomplished photographer, she was eager to shoot pictures showing various stages in the development of insects).

After graduation from Plainfield High School in 1921, she entered Columbia University with the intention of studying art. Here she took a two-hour-a-week course under Clarence H. White, known at the time for his interest in aesthetic photography. After only one semester, Margaret left Columbia following the death of Joseph White. Margaret first used a 3¼×4¼ secondhand Ica Reflex camera with a cracked lens—the crack being of little consequence when she was trying to get photos that resembled paintings. The knowledge imparted by White was put to use when she took a job as the photography and nature counselor at a camp in Connecticut and on the side made money selling picture postcards of subjects she photographed.

The academic year 1922–23 saw her at Ann Arbor, her expenses paid by a man and his sister who were philanthropically inclined. At the University of Michigan she studied herpetology and took photographs for the student yearbook. She was soon dating Everett Chapman, an engineering student who was also earning money as a photographer and had picked up enough to teach Margaret a little. Despite Chapman's demanding mother, who did not approve, they were married in 1924. The next year the couple moved to Indiana. Chapman continued his work at Purdue University

110

while Margaret studied paleontology. But very soon it was apparent that the union was headed for divorce. Margaret had many lovers during her life, but she did not remarry until 1939.

Her eclectic education continued at Western Reserve University at night while she worked during the day at the Cleveland Natural History Museum. By 1927, she had obtained a bachelor's degree from Cornell University where she spent the senior year of her patchwork undergraduate education (she even had credits for swimming and aesthetic dancing from Rutgers).

In need of funds, she got together a collection of photos of the picturesque Ithaca campus. They sold surprisingly well, reinforcing the decision she had made some time before to become a professional photographer. The characteristics that marked Margaret's life were already present. She was resourceful, innovative, determined, and hardworking; she valued independence; she would not allow herself to be deterred from whatever she had set out to do. A black-and-white publicity photo taken around this time shows a trim, attractive, well-dressed young woman (she admitted to loving clothes) behind a large press-type camera mounted on a tripod. Her expressive eyes are noteworthy.

Margaret returned to Cleveland in 1927 to start the Bourke-White Studio. In the beginning, this was in her own apartment, with kitchenette and bathtub doing double duty as parts of a film-processing unit. At this time, she hyphenated her middle and maiden names and henceforth was known as Margaret Bourke-White. The double-barreled name seemed to add prestige to the new studio.

By the mid-1920s, there was among some young people an attitude almost of reverence for the technology that had in the past exerted and was still exerting such powerful influence on American life. In keeping with this, Margaret felt that industry "had evolved an unconscious beauty—often a hidden beauty that was waiting to be discovered." She dreamed of portraying in photographs this beauty and in particular the grandeur of producing steel. But that for the time being would have to be a secondary project. To make ends meet, she began her new career by concentrating on architectural subjects, photos of which could be used in advertisements. She systematically visited potential clients, showed samples of her work, and often came away with orders for photos.

Margaret was fortunate in making friends with Alfred Bemis, a middle-aged man who worked in a camera store. He apparently recognized her talent and seriousness of purpose, and did much to help her. He gave technical advice, lent her equipment, made her an enlarger, and put her in touch with salespeople who knew about the latest in photographic materials.

A stroke of luck was gaining Cleveland's Union Trust Bank as an enthusiastic client. She persuaded its president to introduce her to the president of Otis Steel Company. "I think your pictures of flower gardens are very artistic," the latter told Margaret, "but how can you find anything in my mill?" Her answer was "Please try me."

He gave her the opportunity she was seeking. There were all sorts of difficulties to overcome, such as extremes of light and shade and the high temperatures that blistered a camera's varnish. At the time, there was very little latitude in film and paper; there were no flashbulbs, no strobes, no miniature cameras. Even if the state of the art had been more advanced, no one had had experience in photographing a steel mill. By being there almost every night for a whole winter, often producing nothing satisfactory, she began to have success. Through Bemis she met a salesman who supplied magnesium flares that improved the lighting. Bemis also had a friend who donated some printing paper with an improved emulsion and taught Margaret fine points about the technique of printing.

At last she had a series that satisfied her. She decided to charge $100 per photo—all the film shot for failures, along with the hours spent in experimenting had to be paid for. The president of Otis Steel bought eight photos and commissioned eight more. A photo of the company's 200-ton ladle for molten steel won an award from the Cleveland Art Museum. Margaret Bourke-White had produced unique and artistic photos of an industrial process; she was on her way to fame.

The Otis Steel pictures reached various parts of the country, including New York City. They impressed Henry Luce of *Time* magazine enough to hire Margaret for his new magazine of business and industry, still in the planning stage. For eight months she worked on projects that would provide material for *Fortune* magazine when it began continuous publication. The subjects included shoemaking in Lynn, Massachusetts; glassmaking in Corning, New York; orchid raising in New Jersey; Atlantic-coast fishing; and South Bend, Indiana, as an industrial center. At this period, she often used a 5×7 Corona View camera with an extra bellows extension to accommodate various Bausch and Lomb lenses. Her tripod had a tilt-top head, and she had 1,000-watt Johnson Vent Lites for illumination.

While the United States began to experience the first effects of the 1929 stock-market crash, Margaret was photographing the construction of the Chrysler Building. Working in subfreezing weather at 800 feet above street level on a tower that could sway as much as eight feet did not bother her too much, she wrote years later. The skyscraper intrigued her so much that she eventually moved the Bourke-White Studio to its 61st floor where she often crawled out on a stainless-steel gargoyle "to take pictures of the changing moods of the city." That penthouse became home to two pet alligators and an assortment of turtles.

Margaret was doing well. Her financial arrangement with Luce allowed her to devote half her time to private commissions, which still brought in good money, and the *Fortune* assignments were providing her with the kind of work she craved.

In 1930, she became the first foreign photographer permitted to portray the progress being made under Stalin's first Five Year Plan (1929–1933) to turn the Soviet agrarian economy into an industrial one. She returned to Russia in 1930 and again in 1932. Covering thousands of miles, she took hundreds of photos. Here are some examples: a nursery for the children of auto workers, a premiere ballerina, a textile mill, Georgian women eating borscht, the world's largest blast furnace, a children's clinic.

The excursions to Russia enhanced Margaret's fame. Her *Eyes on Russia* came out in 1931, establishing her as a photojournalist. She was certainly not the first; for example, we mentioned earlier how Jacob Riis's essays and photographs in *How the Other Half Lives* portrayed life in the slums of New York City. Margaret had proved that her photography was superb. Her book showed that she could write well. (Her autobiography was published in 1963. Although it reveals what she wanted known and omits what she did not want known, it is not only fascinating from the standpoint of her activities but shows a mastery of writing.)

As a journalist, however, she left herself open to criticism for her portrayal of Russia. Sean Callahan, editor of the 1972 book *The Photographs of Margaret Bourke-White,* noted that her 135 pages of text were entertaining but pointed out a deficiency in it and her subsequent series of six articles for *New York Times Magazine.* "Nowhere in her studies," he wrote, "is there evidence of the labor camps, the suffering and the terror that was also an integral part of Stalinist Russia."

After a few years at the Chrysler Building, Margaret was in need of a larger studio for her staff. She moved to a skyscraper on Fifth Avenue. She had good advertising accounts, and she gave lectures, but she was in debt. This was partly because of the economic climate that prevailed but also because of poor management on her part.

For food advertisements in particular she was using color photography. She found it generally too complicated, for the most part abandoning it after 1934. In the 1950s, when the state of the art had advanced considerably, she gave it more serious consideration.

Fortune assigned Margaret to cover a dust bowl that was created during the 1930s from the Texas Panhandle to the Dakotas. With only a short time until deadline, she chartered an ancient two-seater plane to cover the area quickly. One of her stark photos taken in South Dakota shows stunted corn bent by the wind and growing in parched cracked soil. She discovered that "right here in my own country there were worlds about which I knew almost nothing." The dust-bowl experience stirred in her a new social consciousness.

In 1935, she did aerial photography for TWA and Eastern Airlines. A photographer who shared her studio instructed her and lent her necessary equipment. The next year she decided to refuse some high-paying advertising offers and to concentrate more on projects that would satisfy a "great need to understand [my] fellow Americans better." That summer she had photographed the presidential candidates, including Earl Browder, head of the American Communist Party. The portrait was run in the *New York Times,* incurring the displeasure of the Newspaper Enterprize Association. She had freelanced when working under an exclusive contract with NEA. As a result, this was terminated. Association with Communists was not to be tolerated, even if it meant no Bourke-White photos.

It was not too long before an attractive opportunity presented itself. Erskine Caldwell, the author of the controversial *Tobacco Road* and a Southerner, wanted to show through a factual book with photographs that his recent novel had presented a genuine picture. This was the sort of project that appealed to Margaret's newly attained social conscience. He and Margaret combined forces for two months, beginning in the summer of 1936. In Caldwell's Ford they covered the cotton-growing states of the Deep South.

Much of the poverty in the rural South was attributed to sharecropping, a practice that dated back to the time of Reconstruction. Plantation owners divided their estates into small one-family farms to be rented for a share of the cotton crop. For what often turned out to be generations, a family risked depletion of the soil, weather uncertainty, the boll weevil, blight, and so on to pay the rent in cotton. By the 1930s, the system had impoverished or indebted millions of Southern farmers.

Margaret's camera caught the suffering on the face of a tobacco farmer, a black sharecropper, a white sharecropper. It reflected the harsh reality of the people's lives, suggesting a land of bleakness and frustration. The collaboration resulted in *You Have Seen Their Faces.* During their sweep through the South, these collaborators began a liaison, although Caldwell was married at the time.

Henry Luce started yet another magazine—*Life,* which began in 1936. Whereas text was primary in *Fortune, Life* would depend more or less on *photos* to tell the story. Margaret and four members of her staff were transferred to the new venture. Her own studio was disbanded, *Life* using most of her photographic equipment to start its own lab. Incidentally, Margaret often had a battery of assistants to carry heavy equipment and set up her lighting arrangements. By this time, flashbulbs were available, a step forward.

Margaret was sent to Montana to shoot construction of Fort Peck Dam, earth-filled, one of several constructed under Roosevelt's New Deal to bring power and irrigation storage to various areas of the country. *Life's* first issue contained Margaret's cover picture of the dam and a group of her other photos described by the magazine as "a human document of American frontier life."

As one of four *Life* photographers, Margaret was enthusiastic about her job. "I'm hardly back in New York," she wrote a friend, "before a new assignment takes me away again." One of these assignments took her to the Arctic Circle in 1937. On the way home with an Anglican bishop and a British composer–travel writer, she chartered a small plane. Because of fog, they made a forced landing on an island too remote for radio transmissions to be picked up. Fortunately the weather cleared before their food supply ran out. There was no lack of adventure in the life of Margaret Bourke-White.

Vicki Goldberg's biography of Margaret gives some insight into how Margaret was regarded by coworkers at *Life*. Regarded as the "queen bee," she was not popular. There was much talk of the excessive numbers of exposures she took; one photographer recalled that in the late forties she finally learned from him how to use a light meter. Nevertheless, for years she had been producing outstanding photographs.

At Simon and Schuster, her publisher, someone mentioned that "everyone was her messenger boy." Peggy Sargent, Margaret's secretary for a time and later photo editor at *Life*, told Goldberg, "One thing I learned above all else from Margaret Bourke-White is the kind of woman I didn't want to be, that centered in myself, that lacking in human relationships, that selfish." Clearly Margaret could be difficult. It is also clear that she was a perfectionist, and even her detractors usually praised her work.

North of the Danube was a second collaborative work by Caldwell and Bourke-White. It was based on material they had collected during their travels in Czechoslovakia in 1938 when Germany was threatening to annex the Sudetenland, a region in northern Czechoslovakia (at Munich on September 29–30, France and Great Britain, hoping to avoid war with Hitler, were behind an ultimatum to Czechoslovakia to cede the Sudetenland to Germany by October 10).

Margaret married Caldwell in 1939, despite some serious doubts. She succeeded in having him sign a marriage contract. At that time, there was still some prejudice about the employment of married women. Margaret expressed her opinion on this when she was invited to contribute to a magazine article entitled "The Married Woman in Business." She wrote, "No democracy can afford to arrest the mental development of women by forcing them to give up outside work upon marriage, nor should it deprive itself of the enriching effect of the work performed by its married women."

Beginning in 1940 and continuing for the next 15 years, the Federal Bureau of Investigation pursued an undercover investigation of Margaret's activities. It is presumed that this was because she had affiliations with some so-called Communist-front organizations. It was also in 1940 that she and her new husband gathered material for what would be the third and last book they would write together—*Say, Is This the U.S.A.?*

In the early 1940s, Margaret's interest in Russia was related to her expressed desire to photograph war. By 1941, much of Europe had fallen to the Nazis. Russia was still their ally, but one of the editors of *Life* and Margaret and Caldwell believed that the nonaggression pact notwithstanding, Germany was about to double-cross Russia by attacking her. So Margaret was dispatched to the Soviet Union. Caldwell was eager to go too since his works had been well received by the Russians. Because of the German occupation of many European countries, they reached their destination via the Pacific Ocean and China. Their premonition had been right. Exactly one month after their arrival, Germany invaded Russia.

When Moscow was bombed, Margaret was the only American photographer in that city. She made the most of the opportunity. When officials at the American Embassy realized that she intended to stay, they extended their help (she once dispatched film to *Life* via Harry Hopkins, Roosevelt's personal envoy to Russia).

Although she held a special photographer's pass, she was required to go to air-raid shelters with everyone else, except when she used the embassy roof. Many of her photos were shot from the balcony of their historic hotel suite where Trotsky and later the Lindberghs had once stood and looked out at the Kremlin. According to Margaret, "The hotel suite possessed a Czarist magnificence. Cupids swung from the chandelier, and the drawing room was furnished with a grand piano, a great white bear rug, and many statuettes of Ural Mountain marble. Its prominent feature was a gold-fluted pillar bearing on its summit a bust of Napoleon." Securing the art objects in the suite was a necessary preparation for night bombing. She recounted: "The Napoleon pillar was too heavy to move, and in the darkness and the vibration, I feared Napoleon more than Hitler."

Since Caldwell made radio broadcasts to the United States, Margaret was sometimes alone in the evenings. She dodged air-raid wardens who sought to evacuate the building when the sirens sounded. She recalled that at times their search was in progress while she was developing photos. She seems to have been as concerned about whether these would be overdeveloped while she was in hiding as she was about the bombing. Her developing trays were kept in the bathtub, and she strung film to dry from cords stretched back and forth between the bathroom water pipes or pinned to window curtains and so on.

In her autobiography, Margaret described graphically her experience in shooting the bombing from her balcony: "Once I began viewing the skyline through the ground glass of the camera, my world became one of composing streaks and dashes of light, of judging the lengths of exposures,

Margaret Bourke-White photographing a German bomber on exhibition, shot down by the Russians. Courtesy of Library of Congress.

of trying to make each sheet of film bring out the most dramatic portions of the spectacles of lights unfolding before the lens." One absolutely spectacular photo silhouettes the Kremlin against a sky streaked with the paths of tracer bullets and illuminated by numerous parachute flares.

Here is more on how Margaret operated:

> I would creep out on the balcony quietly so as not to attract the attention of the soldiers on guard in Red Square below, and place two cameras shooting in opposite directions so they would cover as much of the sky as possible. Usually I set two additional cameras with telephoto lenses on the wide marble windowsill. How I used them would depend on the size of the raid. To me, the severity of the raid was measured by whether it was a two-camera, three-camera, or four-camera night. But I never operated all five cameras at once. My fifth camera I transferred to the Embassy basement. The possibility of being left without a single camera grew to be an obsession, so I took care to divide the risk.

The pair remained in Russia through its first four months of war. Margaret was able to supply *Life* with material that portrayed the life of the people during that period. Personally, she was most interested in the changes she encountered since her visit 10 years previously. They visited the front, which was then near Smolensk, and Margaret was permitted to photograph Stalin.

With the Russian winter approaching, they obtained passage home on a British troopship, part of a convoy that sailed from Archangel via the Arctic Ocean to Glasgow, a 15-day journey. Occupied Europe made such an out-of-the-way route necessary. Air travel was available from Scotland.

Back home, Margaret wrote *Shooting the Russian War* and gave lectures. Her remarks at a panel discussion showed that she had gained insight into some of the nation's problems:

> If our democracy is going to continue, it must provide for the people as well as if not better than the totalitarian states do in terms of certain basic commodities: healthful conditions, adequate education and economic welfare.... Our country lacks some of the aspects of democracy when colored people who must pay taxes as regularly as their white neighbors derive such dissimilar benefits.

Caldwell had an offer from Hollywood and saw to it that Margaret too would receive a good one. He wanted her to live with him in their Arizona home; he also wanted a child. His moods had always been hard for her to deal with. He was especially jealous of *Life*. "There was a terrible jealousy of my work, which he understood very well," she observed. "He loved my work and he encouraged me in it except that he wanted to make the choices. But if *Life*'s editors made the choice, he couldn't stand it. He would oppose

Margaret Bourke-White during World War II. Courtesy of National Archives.

it and find some way to undermine it." With invasion of Europe in the offing, she was determined to go overseas, not to wait out the war in Arizona. Their differences seemed irreconcilable. Margaret would not be dominated, so Erskine sued for divorce.

Life arranged with the military for Margaret to be accredited to the U.S. Army Air Corps as a war correspondent, her pictures to be used by both the Air Corps and the magazine. Her first rank was lieutenant, and at war's end she was a lieutenant colonel.

The summer of 1942 found her in England covering the arrival of the first 13 B-17s that would bomb Germany. Her request to go on a bombing mission was turned down, although male journalists were permitted. She was allowed to photograph Churchill on his 68th birthday (she had shot him in 1940 as well) and also Haile Selassie, the Emperor of Ethiopia in exile in London.

Through General Jimmy Doolittle, Margaret had obtained permission to go to North Africa where the invasion of Europe was shaping up. Since transport there by a Flying Fortress was considered too dangerous for her, she was ordered to a convoy. Ironically, the ship she was aboard was torpedoed en route to Algiers. Margaret found herself in the same lifeboat as Kay Summersby, Ike's attractive military chauffeur. In a Bourke-White photo taken after a night in that boat, the survivors are shown waving at the British search plane that spotted them and sent a destroyer to the rescue. Margaret seldom missed a photo opportunity.

After the torpedoing, the brass no longer held out. Terming it "what was to be the greatest experience of my life," Margaret received a green light to fly over a target in a B-17. The plane was unpressurized, and since she would be required to wear electric mittens when an altitude of 15,000 feet was reached, she would have to shoot her photos below 15,000. The bomber took off from a secret spot in the Sahara Desert, its mission to destroy the El Alouina airfield at Tunis, an area from which the Germans ferried troops from Sicily. The pilot was Major Paul Tibbetts, who would later fly the *Enola Gay* over Hiroshima. The raid was successful, ridding North Africa of the Luftwaffe. It was also the first bombing mission with a woman accompanying the Air Corps crew. We should mention that in such situations, all her pictures and text went to a censor before delivery to *Life*.

Margaret's next assignment was Italy. In 1943, she covered Army Supply Services and later shot scenes around Naples and Casino Valley. Much of the material was used in her 1944 book, *Purple Heart Valley*.

She was with Patton's Third Army in the spring of 1945, when she saw the horror of the death camps. Although "The Living Dead of Buchenwald" is considered a classic in the history of photography, the scenes she took at Number 3 Erla Work Camp (for the Leipzig Mochau aircraft factory) are more unusual — and grisly. Her words describe the brutal atrocity behind them:

> The bodies were still smoldering when we got there, terribly charred but still in human form. We learned the ghastly details from one of the few survivors. The SS had made use of a simple expedient to get rid of the inmates all at once. The SS guards made pails of steaming soup, and as soon as the inmates were all inside the mess hall, the SS put blankets over the windows, threw in hand grenades and pailfuls of a blazing acetate solution. The building went up in sheets of flame. Some escaped, only to die, human torches on the high barbed-wire fence. Even those who were successful in scaling the fence were picked off as they ran across an open field by savage youngsters of the Hitler *Jugend* shooting from a tank. There had been three hundred inmates; there were eighteen who miraculously survived.

During this stint, she made a first-rate portrait of a helmeted General Patton in uniform. In *Dear Fatherland, Rest Quietly*, Margaret described the end of the conflict and postwar conditions in Germany. (*The Taste of War* is an anthology of her war memoirs edited by Jonathan Silverman and drawn from three of her books: *Shooting the Russian War, Purple Heart Valley*, and *Dear Fatherland, Rest Quietly*.)

Peace did not end Margaret's foreign assignments. It was her lot between 1946 and 1948 to witness the turmoil associated with India's gaining independence. Muslims wanted Pakistan to become a separate state. Hindus opposed this. Bloody conflict followed, with terrible suffering and loss of life. Regarding violence in Calcutta, she wrote:

> The streets were literally strewn with dead bodies, an officially estimated six thousand, but I myself saw many more. Scattered between bodies of men were the bodies of their animals. Countless cows, swollen with heat, were as dead as their masters.... In Calcutta, a city larger than Detroit, vast areas were dark with ruins and black with the wings of vultures that hovered impartially over the Hindu and Muslim dead. Like Germany's concentration camps, this was the ultimate result of racial and religious prejudice.

Her "Gandhi at His Spinning Wheel" is well known; her portrait of Nehru shows a pensive man; her photos of the refugees are masterpieces. In *Halfway to Freedom* Margaret recounted her Indian experiences.

Between 1945 and 1950, she was in South Africa. Her photos of gold miners are outstanding. She wrote scathingly of the official practice of separating the races. She later expressed herself about the photographer's dilemma when such issues present themselves. "What are the ethics of a photographer in a situation like this?" she asked. "You need people's help to get permission to make arrangements; you are dependent on the good will of those around you. Perhaps they think you share their point of view. However angry you are, you cannot jeopardize your official contacts by denouncing an outrage before you have photographed it."

When the Korean War came, Margaret's chief interest was the South Koreans who fought the Communists as guerrillas. At this time, she began to use miniature Japanese-made Nikon cameras.

By 1953 she was experiencing the first symptoms of a degenerative and progressive disease of the nervous system. It would be almost 20 years before she died, but gradually the condition curtailed her physical activity. It did not prevent her from writing her autobiography, which she worked on for some eight years at the beautiful home she and Caldwell had purchased in Darien, Connecticut. Before her illness, both Rutgers University and the University of Michigan bestowed honorary doctorates.

Today, drug therapy is available to those who like Margaret suffer from Parkinson's disease. However, that was not available until the late 1960s. In 1959 she had an operation on one side of her brain to control the disease. Two years later, the operation was performed on the opposite side. She allowed publicity about her illness. *Life* ran a feature about her fight against the inroads of the disease, and the story of her operation was shown on television, Theresa Wright playing the lead. Margaret Bourke-White died in 1971 at the age of 67.

In the 1980s, an original Turner Network Television production, *Margaret Bourke-White,* starred Farrah Fawcett in the title role. Today, *Life* Picture Service holds the bulk of Margaret's photos, cataloged and cross-referenced according to subject matter and personality. They can be copied for a fee, and libraries contain books filled with photos taken at various stages of her career. Beginning with steel manufacture and advancing to the portrayal of human emotions, they remain artistic expressions of much of the history of the twentieth century.

If Margaret were beginning her career today, how would she proceed? We cannot know. We do know that she had asked for and received permission from *Life* to go to the moon when space flight had advanced sufficiently to permit that. Surely she would now be making spectacular television pictures of Earth's neighbors in outer space.

Alfred Eisenstaedt, a distinguished photographer who was a colleague and friend of Margaret, gave her this tribute in 1982:

> Being female did not discourage her from doing exactly what she wanted to do. And what she did, she did brilliantly.... Maggie's contributions to photography are considerable. But her dedication and determination to show the world as it is are the qualities by which I remember her most and because of which I can truly say that Margaret Bourke-White was a remarkable person.

Jonathan Silverman, author of *For the World to See: The Life of Margaret Bourke-White,* wrote: "She was a person who lived, above all, to record history, and in documenting the remarkable drama of this century, as she did, secured herself a remarkable place in history as well."

Rachel Carson

Rachel Carson had established herself as a writer with *The Sea Around Us*. With a different type of book *(Silent Spring)*, she interested America and much of the world in the environmental movement.

Rachel Louise Carson was born on May 27, 1907, to Robert Warden and Maria (McLean) Carson, who lived at the edge of Springdale, Pennsylvania, on 65 acres of beautiful undeveloped land. Mr. Carson sold real estate, but the family lived in moderate circumstances. Mrs. Carson was an educated woman who encouraged in Rachel a deep love of nature. She was a dominant influence in her daughter's life, and there seems to have been an unusually strong bond between them.

Rachel attended public schools. After graduation from Parnassus High School in 1925, she won a scholarship of $100 a year toward tuition at Pennsylvania College for Women in nearby Pittsburgh (now Chatham College). Intending to become a writer, she chose an English major. A required course in biology prompted her to consider a career in science, and in the middle of her junior year, she changed her major to zoology. Rachel said later, "It never occurred to me, or apparently to anyone else, that I could combine two careers." She graduated magna cum laude in 1928.

With the aid of a fellowship, Rachel spent that summer, the first of many, at the well-known Marine Biological Laboratory in Woods Hole, Massachusetts. In the fall she began graduate study in zoology at the Johns Hopkins University in Baltimore, receiving a master's degree in 1932.

For several years she held jobs as a teaching or laboratory assistant at Hopkins and for a short time at the University of Maryland. In the midst of the Depression, money was more of a problem than ever, and in 1930 the Carson family moved to a house in Baltimore so she could live at home. Following the death of Robert Carson in 1935, Rachel took part-time work with the U.S. Bureau of Fisheries. Elmer Higgins, head of the Division of Scientific Inquiry, needed a writer familiar enough with marine biology to write radio scripts for a series entitled "Romance Under the Waters."

A short time later, there was another death in the family. Rachel's sister died at 40, leaving two young daughters. Rachel and Mrs. Carson moved them into the house in Silver Spring, Maryland, where mother and daughter were living. Rachel was now responsible for the financial support of the household. Fortunately she soon obtained a federal position at $2,000 a year. She was assigned to Higgins's office.

By this time, she had been published in the Baltimore *Sunday Sun,* having written among other pieces a series on fisheries. When asked to compose "something of a general sort about the sea," she produced such outstanding prose that Higgins suggested she submit it to *Atlantic Monthly.* Her essay, "Undersea," was accepted and proved so impressive that it led to a contract from Simon and Schuster to write *Under the Sea-Wind: A Naturalist's Picture of Ocean Life.* Published in 1941, this narrates the lives of creatures that inhabit the sea, which itself is the book's central character. Despite good reviews from scientists, sales were poor.

In 1940, the Bureaus of Fisheries and Biological Survey merged to form the Fish and Wildlife Service of the Department of the Interior. Rachel advanced in steps from Assistant Aquatic Biologist (1942–1943) to Biologist and Chief Editor (1949–1952). During World War II, one of her tasks was to promote little-known seafoods as sources of protein. Her training and standing in the department put her in a unique position of benefit to her off-the-job writing. She was in touch with ongoing research and authorities. In fact, she had above-average knowledge relating to the scientific and political problems in her field.

In 1946, Rachel rented a cabin on the Sheepscot River near Boothbay, Maine. Here she wandered on the beach, spending most of her time studying nature. She wrote a friend, "My greatest ambition is to be able to buy a place here and then manage to spend a great deal of time in it—summers at least!" That ambition was realized seven years later when she built a cottage in West Southport, Maine.

"The book I am writing is something I have had in mind for a good while," Rachel wrote in 1948. "I have had to wait to undertake it until at least a part of the wartime oceanographic studies should be published, for I wanted to reflect some of the new concepts of the ocean that research has developed. Now there seems to be enough to go ahead on."

The book was *The Sea Around Us.* After its publication, she explained, "[At Woods Hole] I could see the racing tidal currents pouring through the 'Hole' or watch the waves breaking at Nobska Point after a storm, and there I first became really aware of the unseen ocean currents, the masses of drifting sargassum weed that would come in from the distant Gulf Stream after a storm, and tropical creatures like the beautiful Portuguese man-of-war were carried in from the warm rivers offshore." She wrote of the library research involved: "I believe I consulted at a minimum, somewhat more than a thousand separate printed sources. In addition to this, I corresponded with oceanographers all over the world and personally discussed the book with many specialists."

Rachel chose as her agent Marie Rodell, who was also a writer, and by June 1949, a contract with Oxford University Press had been obtained.

That same summer, she tried undersea diving in Florida but only to a depth of 15 feet. She and her agent also spent 10 days on a research vessel that was being used in a study of deep-sea commercial fishing around Georges Bank.

The manuscript of *The Sea Around Us* was delivered in July 1950. In discussing the design of the book, Rachel wrote to the editor of her concern that "the book should be dismissed as another 'introduction to oceanography.'" To prevent that impression, she made suggestions regarding the layout. Katherine S. Howe made the drawings.

Rodell sold a prepublication chapter entitled "The Birth of an Island" to the *Yale Review*. This ultimately earned the George Westinghouse Science Writing Award of the American Association for the Advancement of Science. The *New Yorker* used an advance copy to run approximately half of the material as a three-part piece, "Profile of the Sea."

Publication day was July 2, 1951. By September 9, *The Sea Around Us* was on the *New York Times* bestseller list and would remain there for 86 weeks. The book is a tribute to Rachel's ability to weave scientific and historical facts into an artistic presentation. A few passages show the style.

It is a confused pattern that the waves make in the open sea — a mixture of countless different wave trains, intermingling, overtaking, passing, or sometimes engulfing one another; each group differing from the others in the place and manner of its origin, in its speed, its direction of movement; some doomed never to reach any shore, others destined to roll across half an ocean before they dissolve in thunder on a distant beach.
• • • •
The plants and animals of the sea are very much better chemists than men, and so far our own efforts to extract the mineral wealth of the sea have been feeble compared with those of lower forms of life. They have been able to find and to utilize elements present in such minute traces that human chemists could not detect their presence until, very recently, highly refined methods of spectroscopic analysis were developed.
• • • •
For the sea lies all about us. The commerce of all lands must cross it. The very winds that move over the lands have been cradled on its broad expanse and seek ever to return to it. The continents themselves dissolve and pass to the sea in grain after grain of eroded land. So the rains that rose from it return again in rivers. In its myserious past it encompasses all the dim origins of life and receives in the end after, it may be, many transmutations, the dead husks of that same life. For all at last returns to the sea — to Oceanus, the ocean river, like the ever-flowing stream of life, the beginning and the end.

The Sea Around Us won the National Book Award for the best nonfiction book of 1951 and the John Burroughs Medal for a natural-history book of outstanding literary quality. Foreign translations were issued, as well as junior editions. Among other honors, *The Sea Around Us* brought its author four honorary degrees. RCA-Victor had her write album notes for Debussy's *La Mer,* conducted by Arturo Toscanini. An RKO documentary film based on her book was not to Rachel's liking, but it won an Oscar.

To her liking, however, was the award of a Guggenheim Fellowship to write another book. *The Sea* brought another bonus. After buying the rights to *Under the Sea-Wind* from Simon and Schuster, Oxford reissued it. This book too made the bestseller list. The royalties from *The Sea Around Us* enabled Rachel to resign her government position and devote herself full-time to writing. *The Edge of the Sea* appeared in 1955. With black-and-white pencil drawings done by Fish and Wildlife staff artist Bob Hines, it sold well and brought new honors.

Rachel had never married. In 1957, she adopted her five-year-old grandnephew Roger Christie when his mother died. The latter was Rachel's niece Marjorie, who had been brought up by Rachel and her mother (the little boy had lost his father too). Rachel taught Roger, as she had taught Marjorie before him, to appreciate the wonders of nature.

The previous year, she had written a friend, "Next, I'm committed to write an article for the *Woman's Home Companion.* It's about encouraging awareness of nature in children, the working title being 'Teach Your Child to Wonder.'" Explaining about Roger, she continued, "I have had a bit of experience through a very young nephew who has visited me in Southport each summer since he was 18 months old, and the *Companion* editors, true to editorial habit of thought, wish me to 'personalize' (horrid word!) the piece as much as possible in terms of Roger." After her death, the text of the magazine article, illustrated with photographs, appeared as *The Sense of Wonder,* published by Harper and Row.

As a biologist, Rachel regarded as ominous any process that might upset the delicate balance of nature. As far back as 1945, she had offered to write for *Reader's Digest* a timely story on the use of DDT but had been turned down.

The Swiss chemist Paul Müller had discovered in 1939 that DDT (*d*ichlorodiphenyl*t*richlorethane) was an effective insecticide. The compound, which had been synthesized many years before, was relatively inexpensive and had been used successfully against insects that attack valuable crops. It had also destroyed lice, fleas, and mosquitoes; vectors, respectively, of typhus and plague and of malaria and yellow fever. During and immediately following World War II, for example, delousing with DDT had aborted serious outbreaks of typhus, contrasting markedly with the situation in World War I when more than 2 million lives were lost to that disease. After the Second World War, DDT was responsible for a significant drop in the worldwide incidence of malaria. The chemical's performance brought Müller the 1948 Nobel Prize in physiology and medicine.

But DDT had serious drawbacks. It was found that many species of insects rapidly developed populations resistant to it. In addition, the highly stable compound accumulated in insects that were eaten by other animals, with the result that certain birds and fishes experienced severe toxic effects that caused death. Later there was evidence that DDT was a carcinogen.

As DDT and other chemicals related and unrelated to it became widely used in agriculture, some scientists warned of the dangers. Little attention was paid them, even by the scientific community and certainly by the laity. *The Sea Around Us* had given Rachel an excellent track record for communicating scientific facts to the layman, and in 1958 she decided to expose to her reading public the harm involved in the indiscriminate use of pesticides.

She was quite aware that her task would not be easy. She would need to back up every statement. She would antagonize vested interests like the chemical and food-processing industries and government agencies like the Department of Agriculture. "But," she said later, "knowing the facts as I did, I could not rest until I had brought them to public attention."

Rachel's crusade was given a start by an incident in Duxbury, Massachusetts. There Olga Huckins and her husband had a private bird sanctuary that had suffered from the state's aerial-spraying program designed to control mosquitoes. Many of the sanctuary birds as well as harmless insects had died—and the mosquitoes still persisted. Since more spraying was planned by the state, Mrs. Huckins sought Rachel's advice about where help from Washington might be sought.

According to Rachel, "I began to look around for the information she wanted, and the more I learned about the use of pesticides the more appalled I became. I realized that here was the material for a book." The book was not published as soon as she had planned. Rachel proceeded in her usual fashion of evaluating the literature and consulting experts. Knowledge in the area was evolving rapidly, and the process became very time-consuming.

Another problem presented itself: Oxford University Press needed a revision of *The Sea Around Us*. Rachel solved that by adding a section of notes that revised the statistical information and noted the most important discoveries since the first edition. Even with good secretarial assistance, this was a demanding task.

To complicate matters, Rachel was beset with personal problems. Maria Carson, her mother, died in December 1958. She lived until she was close to 90 and during the last years of her life had required much care. Rachel was becoming handicapped with arthritis. In the spring of 1960, she

Rachel Carson, about 1962. Courtesy of Curator of American Literature, Beinecke Rare Book and Manuscript Library, Yale University.

had surgery for cancer of the breast. Some months later, it was necessary for her to undergo radiation therapy. Late in the year she wrote her editor that treatments would mean a "pretty serious diversion of time and capacity for work. . . . Perhaps even more than ever, I am eager to get the book done."

Some of the strain was reflected in a letter written to a friend in 1961: "I am working late at night most of the time now. If I can fight off the desire to go to bed around 11:30 I seem to get my second wind and be able to go on. . . . What lies beneath the most important part of this chapter is a whole field of the most technical and difficult biology—discoveries only recently made. How to reveal enough to give understanding to the most serious effects of the chemicals without being technical, how to simplify without error—these have been the problems of rather monumental proportions."

The new book was to be published by Houghton Mifflin. It was Paul Brooks, its editor in chief, who suggested *Silent Spring* as the title. Keats's lines

> The sedge is wither'd from the lake,
> And no birds sing.

were used on the motto page, thanks to Marie Rodell. The dedication read:

> To Albert Schweitzer
> who said
> "Man has lost the capacity to foresee
> and to forestall. He will end by
> destroying the earth."

Attractive illustrations done by Lois and Louis Darling served to dispel any impression that *Silent Spring* was a textbook.

Previous to the issue of the book, a serialization appeared in the *New Yorker*, beginning June 16, 1962. While the material for the book was at the printer, Velsicol Corporation in Chicago threatened suit, claiming there was in the serialization an inaccurate statement about their product Choldane. Houghton Mifflin refused to change the statement. No suit ensued.

The passages below give flavor of the book.

> The world of systemic insecticides is a weird world, surpassing the im-
> aginings of the brothers Grimm—perhaps most closely akin to the car-
> toon world of Charles Addams. It is a world where the enchanted forest
> of the fairy tales has become the poisonous forest in which an insect that
> chews a leaf or sucks the sap of a plant is doomed. It is a world where
> a flea bites a dog, and dies because the dog's blood had been made
> poisonous, where an insect may die from vapors emanating from a plant
> it has never touched, where a bee may carry poisonous nectar back to its
> hive and presently produce poisonous honey.
>
> • • • •
>
> Rain, falling on the land, settles down through pores and cracks in soil
> and rock, penetrating deeper and deeper until eventually it reaches a
> zone where all the pores of the rock are filled with water, a dark, subsur-
> face sea, rising under hills, sinking beneath valleys. This groundwater is
> always on the move, sometimes at a pace so slow that it travels no more
> than 50 feet a year, sometimes rapidly, by comparison, so that it moves
> nearly a tenth of a mile in a day. It travels by unseen waterways until here
> and there it comes to the surface as a spring, or perhaps it is tapped to
> feed a well. But mostly it contributes to streams and so to rivers. Except

for what enters streams directly as rain or surface runoff, all the running water on the earth's surface was at one time groundwater. And so, in a very real and frightening sense, pollution of the groundwater is pollution of water everywhere.

• • • •

Insects, so essential to our agriculture and indeed to our landscape as we know it, deserve something better from us than the senseless destruction of their habitat. Honey bees and wild bees depend heavily on such "weeds" as goldenrod, mustard, and dandelions for pollen that serves as the food of their young. Vetch furnishes essential spring forage for bees before the alfalfa is in bloom, tiding them over for this early season so that they are ready to pollinate the alfalfa. In the fall they depend on goldenrod at a season when no other food is available, to stock up for the winter. By the precise and delicate timing that is nature's own, the emergence of one species of wild bees takes place on the very day of the opening of the willow blossoms. There is no dearth of men who understand these things, but these are not the men who order the wholesale drenching of the landscape with chemicals.

• • • •

Who has made the decision that sets in motion these chains of poisonings, this ever-widening wave of death that spreads out, like ripples when a pebble is dropped into a still pond? Who has placed in one pan of the scales the leaves that might have been eaten by the beetles and in the other the pitiful heaps of the many-hued feathers, the lifeless remains of the birds that fell before the unselective bludgeon of insecticidal poisons? Who has decided—who has the *right* to decide—for the countless legions of people who were not consulted that the supreme value is a world without insects, even though it be also a sterile world ungraced by the curving wing of a bird in flight?

• • • •

For each of us, as for the robin in Michigan or the salmon in the Miramichi, this is a problem of ecology, of interrelationships, of interdependence. We poison the caddis flies in a stream and the salmon runs dwindle and die. We poison the gnats in a lake and the poison travels from link to link of the food chain and soon the birds of the lake margins become its victims. We spray our elms and the following springs are silent of robin song, not because we sprayed the robins directly but because the poison traveled, step by step, through the now familiar elm leaf-earthworm-robin cycle. These are matters of record, observable, part of the visible world around us. They reflect the web of life—or death—that scientists know as ecology.

• • • •

We see with an understanding eye only if we have walked in the garden at night and here and there with a flashlight have glimpsed the mantis stealthily creeping upon her prey. Then we sense something of the drama of the hunter and the hunted. Then we begin to feel something of that relentlessly pressing force by which nature controls her own.... Thus, through the circumstances of their lives, and the nature of their own wants, all these have been our allies in keeping the balance of nature tilted in our favor. Yet we have turned our artillery against our friends. The terrible danger is that we have grossly underestimated their value by keeping at bay a dark tide of enemies that, without their help, can overrun us.

Two weeks after publication, *Silent Spring* had become a best-seller. Foreign editions were issued, and Rachel received invitations to London and Uppsala, Sweden. These she was forced to decline because of poor health. Criticism came from the quarters she had anticipated, but the overwhelming approval of both scientists and laity pleased her. Paul Brooks, her editor and personal friend, has emphasized that her chief concern was that the book should have a lasting effect on government policy.

Many more honors were bestowed. One that Rachel took particular pride in was election to the American Academy of Arts and Letters. The citation read: "A scientist in the grand literary style of Galileo and Buffon, she has used her scientific knowledge and moral feeling to deepen our consciousness of living nature and to alert us to the calamitous possibility that our short-sighted technological conquests might destroy the very sources of our being. Who could better exemplify the humanist tradition of this Academy?"

Although the inexorable progress of cancer had made inroads on her physical health, Rachel was able to fulfill a long-held desire to see the California redwoods. She died in Silver Spring in 1964 at 56.

In 1971, Secretary of the Interior Walter Hickel dedicated the Rachel Carson National Wildlife Refuge, located on the coast of Maine. Nine years later, the Presidential Medal of Freedom was awarded posthumously to Rachel Carson. Accepting it from President Jimmy Carter was Roger, her adopted son. A Rachel Carson 17-cent postage stamp was issued in 1981.

Robert Downs included *Silent Spring* in his *Books That Changed America,* declaring it comparable in its impact on public consciousness and demand for instant action to Tom Paine's *Common Sense,* Harriet Beecher Stowe's *Uncle Tom's Cabin,* and Upton Sinclair's *The Jungle.*

Rachel's fervent desire that her book would have a lasting effect on government policy was realized. Following *Silent Spring,* President Kennedy appointed a special panel to study the effects of pesticides on the environment. The journal *Science* noted that the panel's report carefully balanced risks versus benefits and that it added up "to a fairly thoroughgoing vindication of Rachel Carson's *Silent Spring* thesis."

Another governmental action was the creation of the Environmental Protection Agency (EPA), in 1970, its purpose "the protection, development and enhancement of the total environment." Many hope that in the not-too-distant future, this agency will attain cabinet status.

In 1970 the Occupational Safety and Health Act (OSHA) was passed "to assure so far as possible every working man and woman in the Nation safe and healthful working conditions." The climate that made possible the EPA contributed to the founding of OSHA.

Rachel recognized that a book like *Silent Spring* would require constant revision. With regard to her graduate training at Hopkins, she noted, "This was the unforgettable lesson: we do not really know anything. What we think we know today is replaced by something else tomorrow." The statistics on this or that pesticide or herbicide will change. They do not constitute the central issue; they were facts used to reinforce her premise. The significance of *Silent Spring*, Rachel's enduring monument, is that it forced ordinary people to think of the future in terms of the environment. It succeeded in doing this because the author was blessed with vision, an analytical mind, a capacity to work hard, and an ability to express herself clearly in graceful prose. The problem of risk versus benefit is paramount and will remain with us, but thanks to Rachel, it will receive more consideration.

She was not the only person responsible for the growth of the environmental movement. Many conservationists had been and continued to be active, but she certainly was a prime mover. Books such as *Since Silent Spring* by Frank Graham, Jr., and more recently H. Patricia Hynes's *The Recurring Silent Spring* point out progress and lack of it.

An oil spill in California in 1969 prompted Gaylord Nelson, then a senator from Wisconsin, to organize the first Earth Day, April 22, 1970. This gave great impetus to the environmental movement, which continues to grow. Terms seldom heard before *Silent Spring* are part of today's vocabulary: *greenhouse effect, recycling, endangered species, food chain, toxic substances, wetlands, organic gardening,* and the like.

For Earth Day 1990, a Green National Pledge Drive was initiated. Signatories agreed to act, buy, vote, and support as follows:

> I pledge to do my best to recycle, conserve energy, save water, use efficient transportation, and make every day as if every day were Earth Day.
> I pledge to try to do business with corporations that act in an environmentally responsible way.
> I pledge to vote and support candidates who demonstrate their true concern for the environment by their actions.
> I pledge to support the passage of local, state and federal laws and international treaties that protect the environment.

Rachel's contribution is well expressed in the citation for the Presidential Medal of Freedom:

> Never silent in the face of destructive trends, Rachel Carson fed a spring of awareness across America and beyond. A biologist with a gentle, clear

voice, she welcomed her audiences to her love of the sea, while with an equally clear determined voice she warned Americans of the dangers human beings themselves pose for their own environment. Always concerned, always eloquent, she created a tide of environmental consciousness that has not ebbed.

Betty Friedan

A 1984 book *The Changing Lives of American Women* stated: "Clearly, work outside the house is no longer limited by traditional obligations of women to their husbands and children. . . . Women entering adulthood are [now] concerned with integrating labor force participation and family responsibility throughout their lives."

This changed attitude was expressed and espoused by Betty Friedan in *The Feminine Mystique*, published in 1963. That book and NOW, the organization Ms. Friedan founded to implement her thesis, remain her enduring monuments.

She was born Betty Naomi Goldstein on February 4, 1921, in Peoria, Illinois. Her ancestry was Jewish. Her father, Harry Goldstein, a jeweler, was a Russian immigrant. Her mother, Miriam (Horowitz) Goldstein, was college educated and had been a newspaperwoman until she married. Betty lived the first 17 years of her life in Peoria, apparently as a typical middle-class midwesterner. Her published writing emphasizes her activities in the women's movement and deals little with her personal background.

After graduating summa cum laude from Smith College in 1942, she had a year of graduate study in psychology at the University of California at Berkeley. Migrating to New York City, Betty worked as a newspaperwoman. She also arranged for abortions—illegal then, of course—for Smith alumnae because "I was a radical, also a psychologist and unshockable." When World War II ended, her job on a small labor-news service was taken by a man recently discharged from the armed services.

By 1947, Betty was married to Carl Friedan. They had met when he returned from Europe where he was running the Soldier Show Company. He was about to start a summer theater in New Jersey. These two eventually became the parents of two sons and a daughter, a future engineer, physicist and physician, whom Betty cherished. After some stays in rented facilities, the family settled in their own 11-room Charles Addams Victorian house on the Hudson River in Rockland County.

Betty continued to work for a short time, taking maternity leave with the advent of her first child. In her words, "Shortly after 1949, I was fired from my job because I was pregnant again. They weren't about to put up with the inconvenience of another year's maternity leave, even though I was *entitled* to it under my union contract. It was *wrong* somehow to fire me just because I was pregnant, and to hire a man instead. I even tried calling a meeting of the people in the union where I worked. It was the first personal stirring of my own feminism, I guess."

For the next eight years, Betty led the life of a middle-class wife and mother. She also did freelance writing for several magazines.

The country was prosperous. Suburbia sheltered countless married women who had either left the work force or had never worked outside the home. With GIs civilians again, larger families were in vogue. To illustrate, when a mother left an obstetrical unit with a new baby, a nurse was likely to remark, "See you next year." Also in that Truman-Eisenhower era, the cold war was casting an increasingly dark shadow, and in 1950–1954, the Korean War was in progress.

The year 1957 saw Betty circulating a Smith College alumnae questionnaire among her classmates. It asked about their experiences and feelings 15 years after leaving their alma mater. Two hundred answered the questions, 89 percent of them housewives.

The replies raised "strange questions about that role we were all then embracing." Apparently these women were not as happy as they appeared; many found life empty and they dreaded the future. The answers from educated affluent housewives and mothers made Betty aware of a "voice within women that says, 'I want something more than my husband and my children and my home.'" She realized that the 1957 glorified image of a woman satisfied with her role at home as wife and mother was spurious. In time Betty named this the *feminine mystique.*

When she submitted an article on her findings, the male editor of *McCall's* rejected it, unconvinced. *Ladies' Home Journal* altered it so drastically that Betty did not permit its publication. *Redbook* turned it down as something with which "only the most neurotic housewife could possibly identify." The upshot of such denial fired her determination to write a book on what she termed "the problem that has no name"—referring to the spiritual malaise imposed on women by circumstances that were in reality very restrictive.

Sometimes Betty took a bus to the New York Public Library where she wrote at a carrel in the Frederick Lewis Allen Room. Sometimes she worked at home when she could find time to herself. She had intended to finish *The Feminine Mystique* in one year; it took five. The actual writing was just one aspect of the project. To develop the topic, she sent out more questionnaires. She interviewed people. She discussed her findings with psychologists, counselors, and other authorities on behavior, and with physicians and clergy. And the book mirrored her own life experiences and reactions.

Published in 1963 by Norton, *The Feminine Mystique* was a best-

Betty Friedan in the 1960s. Courtesy of the Schlesinger Library, Radcliffe College.

seller—and controversial. Through numerous anecdotal descriptions, it portrayed women as leading lives of quiet desperation. Although they were well provided for, they regretted their unfulfilled potential, careers, and the like. Noting that this dissatisfaction existed among wives of both rich and poor, the author stated that "it may not even be felt by women preoccupied with desperate problems of hunger, poverty and illness."

Betty denounced the women's magazines for their part in the campaign to keep women at home. Among many examples, here is one from "How America Lives," *Ladies' Home Journal,* October 1960. A Texas housewife encourages the feminine mystique by proclaiming, "'By 8:30 A.M., when my youngest goes to school, my whole house is clean and neat and I am dressed for the day. I am free to play bridge, attend club meetings, or to stay home and read, listen to Beethoven, and just plain loaf. . . . I am so grateful for my blessings. Wonderful husband, handsome sons with dispositions to match, big comfortable house. . . . I am thankful for my good health and faith in God and such material possessions as two cars, two TV's and two fireplaces.'"

Betty condemned Freud for the damage he caused with his assumption of woman's natural inferiority. Margaret Mead was also censured for advocating adjustment to society as it is found, which would include living within the framework of the conventional cultural definitions of the male and female roles. Betty voiced her belief that women's unhappiness occurred because "our culture does not permit women to accept or gratify their basic need to grow and fulfill their potentialities as human beings, a need which is not solely defined by their sexual role."

She drew attention to the current preoccupation with marriage. She cited a 1962 report by John Bushnel on Vassar College. It showed that a student's "future identity is largely encompassed by the projected role of wife-mother" and that "not only is spinsterhood viewed as a personal tragedy but offspring are considered essential to the full life." So, wrote Betty, "millions of able women in this free land chose, themselves, not to use the door education could have opened for them."

Why did the mystique have such a hold in those postwar years? Here is one of Betty's answers:

> Those who married in the thirties saw their husbands off to war; those who grew up in the forties were afraid, with reason, that they might never have the love, the homes and the children which few women would willingly miss. When the men came back, there was a headlong rush into marriage. The lonely years when husbands or husbands-to-be were away at war—or could be sent away at a bomb's fall—made women particularly vulnerable to the feminine mystique. They were told that the cold dimension of loneliness which the war had added to their lives was the necessary price they had to pay for a career, for any interest outside the home. The mystique spelled out a choice—love, home, children, or other goals and purposes in life. Given such a choice, was it any wonder that so many American women chose love as their whole purpose?

According to Betty, big business helped to keep American women in their homes by supplying useful appliances and promoting them through shrewd advertising. But even with all sorts of laborsaving devices, women seemed to have less free time than ever. Betty explained this by applying Parkinson's law: Work expands to fill the time available. But, she wrote, "no matter how much housework is expanded to fill the time available, it presents little challenge to the adult mind."

Betty contended that the feminine mystique was sometimes responsible for retarding the development of independence in children whose mothers lived vicariously through them.

What could be done to dispel the power of the feminine mystique? Betty's plan was first to see housework for what it is—something to be done as quickly and efficiently as possible. Then it was time to break inside the veil of overglorification of marriage. The next step to get out of the trap was the jump from amateur to professional.

Betty saw the key in lifelong commitment to an art or science, to politics or profession, as necessary. "Such a commitment is not tied to a specific job or locality," she wrote. "It permits year-to-year variation—a full-time paid job in one community, part-time in another, exercise of the professional skill in serious volunteer work or a period of study during pregnancy or early motherhood when a full-time job is not feasible. It is a continuous thread, kept alive by work and study and contacts in the field, in any part of the country."

She further explained: "Women must be educated to a new integration of roles. The more they are encouraged to make that new life plan—integrating a serious lifelong commitment to society with marriage and motherhood—the less conflicts and unnecessary frustrations they will feel as wives and mothers, and the less their daughters will make mistaken choices for lack of a full image of woman's identity."

The last part of the plan (and the book) involved competition.

> She must learn to compete then, not as a woman, but as a human being. Not until a great many women move out of the fringes into the mainstream will society itself provide the arrangements for their new life plan. But every girl who manages to stick it out through law school or medical school, who finishes her M.A. or Ph.D. and goes on to use it, helps others move on. Every woman who fights the remaining barriers to full equality which are masked by the feminine mystique makes it easier for the next woman.

The fame of *The Feminine Mystique* provided Betty with frequent appearances on TV, radio, and the lecture circuit. She thus had a double opportunity to promote the book and more important, her thesis. She traveled extensively throughout the United States and later abroad, becoming in the early years of the women's movement its leading spokesman. Here is an excerpt from a speech she made at the University of California in 1964:

> We must all say yes to ourselves as women, and no to that outworn, obsolete image, the feminine mystique. We must stop denigrating ourselves, stop acquiescing in the remaining prejudices the mystique enshrines. We must recognize and affirm each other in the massiveness of our numbers and our own strength and ask for all women what we all need to move freely ahead. One does not move freely and joyously ahead if one is always torn by conflicts and guilts, nor if one feels like a freak in a man's world, if one is always walking a tightrope between being a good wife and mother and fulfilling one's commitments to society— without help from society. If we ask, I think we can get simple institutional solutions from society to these real problems. Well-run five- or eight-hour-a-day nursery schools or day-care centers are needed, and maternity leaves that are real and not just on paper. . . . Real credit needs to be given for the work you have done as volunteers. More part-time

patterns are needed in all professions for mothers. Above all, women must assume real political equality and take their place as decision-makers in political life.

In 1966, Betty founded the National Organization for Women (NOW). In June the Commission of the Status of Women (originally set up by President John Kennedy at the request of Eleanor Roosevelt) held its annual meeting in Washington, D.C. To 28 women attending, the need for a civil-rights organization for women was clear. At the Hilton Hotel, Betty wrote out on a paper napkin words that would become the keystone of NOW's Statement of Purpose: "to take the actions needed to bring women into the mainstream of American society, now, full equality for women, in fully equal partnership with men."

This Statement of Purpose is the keystone of today's women's movement. In the past, there had been focus on various "women's issues"; now, according to Janet Chafetz and Anthony Dworkin, authors of *Female Revolt*, there was conscious and collective revolt on behalf of women, defined as a general category with a set of problems and needs specific to themselves, which are created by a sociocultural system that categorically disadvantages them relative to males.

Plans were made for an organizational meeting to be held later, and on October 29 NOW became official. The Statement of Purpose that Betty had written was accepted with one deletion; originally she had called for access to birth control and abortion, but that was postponed because it was considered too controversial. Kathryn Clarenbach of the Women's Bureau became chair of the board. Betty was elected president and would hold that office until 1970. Richard Graham was vice president—elected not as a token male but because he had a record of fighting for equality of the sexes. The secretary-treasurer was Caroline Davis of the United Auto Workers. There were 300 charter members; before 1967 ended, there would be 1,200 members. Under Betty's leadership, the organization campaigned for various reforms, such as ending the use of employment notices with a gender requirement, more women in government positions, day-care centers for children, legalized abortion. NOW's support for the Equal Rights Amendment was affirmed.

When *The Feminine Mystique* was published, Betty had few friends or acquaintances who were divorced; apparently there was still some stigma associated with divorce. She stated that she had been considering it for five years, and in 1969 obtained a formal decree.

Betty picked the 50th anniversary of the day that woman's right to vote became part of the Constitution to hold the Women's Strike for Equality. On August 20, 1970, she was among 25,000 who marched along Fifth Avenue in New York City; 10,000 demonstrated in Los Angeles and 15,000 in Chicago. It was Betty's belief that this strike made the power of the women's movement "visible to the world." That same year, she stepped down as NOW's president. New leaders like Gloria Steinem were emerging. It also appeared that Betty did not approve of undue emphasis on single issues—lesbianism in particular. She was considered difficult.

On the personal side, Betty had become part of what she termed a sort of respectable nonhippie commune in East Hampton where she spent many enjoyable weekends and summers, Thanksgivings, and Christmases with congenial friends. This would continue for 10 years.

In 1971 she organized the National Women's Political Caucus, with the intent of supporting political candidates who were behind women's issues. She soon became disillusioned about the motives of some women active in politics: "But there is no guarantee that women will be any purer or less corrupt in their use of power than men."

Betty had always viewed the women's movement as belonging to the mainstream of American society. So rather than writing for the already convinced, especially under a new type of feminist conformity such as she would have encountered with *Ms.*, she had a column in *McCall's* from late 1970 to 1973. She was facing new problems in her life—"the economic burdens of supporting a single-parent family, the loneliness, the need for new roots and new patterns of living." She had no answers, but she would now share the experience honestly with other women in her column, "Betty Friedan's Notebook." Here is a sample:

> Real equality for women has to be an equality of responsibility as well as of privilege and right; that men will be liberated then from the burden of having to hold open the doors, pay all the bills, die ten years younger than women, and fight the wars. I say we can light each other's cigarettes if that means merely that we like each other. If a pregnant woman gets on the bus, of course a man should get up and give her a seat, but if a tired old man gets on the bus, I would give my seat to him. I say that nobody should be drafted to fight this war in Vietnam, or any immoral, unjust war, but any necessary service to society should be assumed by women and men alike; no reason for anyone to be exempt on the basis of sex.

Later she commented on her writing for *McCall's*:

> It not only helped pay for my groceries, it gave me a way to recruit women to the basic goals of equality—to say "you don't have to hate men and renounce motherhood to be a liberated woman"—and thus to help build the women's movement in the largest sense. It also gave me a forum to develop my own idelogy—which is perhaps the ideology of the mainstream of the women's movement—without wasting my energies fighting the extremists who were co-opting the image of "women's lib."

In *The Second Stage,* Betty gave some examples of the thinking of the extremists. For example, man is seen as the enemy; all married women are prostitutes; motherhood and family are oppressors of women; and women would never be free unless the family was abolished.

Betty devoted great energy to support the ERA of 1972:

The Equal Rights Amendment
Complete Text

Section 1.
Equality of rights under the law shall not be denied or abridged by the United States or by any State on account of sex.

Section 2.
The Congress shall have the power to enforce, by appropriate legislation, the provisions of this article.

Section 3.
This amendment shall take effect two years after the date of ratification.

To take effect, ratification by 38 states was necessary. Six years later, with that requirement still unmet, Congress extended the deadline until June 30, 1982. That deadline too passed with insufficient state support—and the proposed amendment died for the time being.

In 1974, Betty organized the Women's Bank and Trust Company in New York City and became one of its directors. Because of her prominence, she taught at many institutions of higher learning, some of them abroad. To prepare herself for lectures, institutes, and so on, she spent much of the years 1973–1976 studying psychology, sociology, and women's history.

Betty's *It Changed My Life: Writings of the Women's Movement* was published by Random House in 1976 (Norton got it out in 1985 with a new author's introduction).

The idea of the superwoman—one who manages to combine successfully and effortlessly her career and wife-mother roles—spurred Betty to write *The Second Stage,* published in 1981 by Summit Books, with a revised edition in 1986. In this book, she noted that the new feminist mystique, denying "that core of women's personhood that is fulfilled through love, nurture, home," was also removed from reality, as was the original feminine mystique. According to Betty, the second stage involves coming to new terms with the family—new terms with love and with work. Men may be at the cutting edge of the second stage.

The second-stage problem is for women and men to be able to choose to have children responsibly, which means not only safe legal medical access to birth control and abortion but maternity and paternity leaves and benefits. Above all, it means really coming to grips with the question of who is going to take care of the child when both mother and father have to share parenting on top of necessary jobs or professional training or commitments.

Among other honors, Betty has received the 1975 Humanist of the Year Award and an honorary degree from Smith College. A current interest is aging.

The Feminine Mystique remains in print. Its basic thesis is hard to deny. Many women become bored unless they are presented challenges. Three of the subjects of this book were not content with the life of a wife and mother: Mary Bethune, Margaret Sanger, and Betty Friedan. Single women like Jane Addams were bored until they found some worthwhile cause to lose themselves in. In contrast, Rachel Carson did not experience such boredom. "There is one quality that characterizes all of us who deal with the sciences of the earth and its life—we are never bored," she explained. "We can't be. There is always something new to be investigated. Every mystery solved brings us to the threshold of a greater one." Few women will involve themselves in scholarly pursuit to the extent that Rachel Carson did, but her life illustrates Betty's contention that challenging and meaningful work can be an antidote to the dissatisfaction that arises when women are overly involved with trivialities. With regard to single women, Betty sought to dispel the belief that forgoing marriage was necessary if a woman was to become truly committed to a career.

Twenty-seven years after the publication of *The Feminine Mystique,* some members of the graduating class of Wellesley College signified their belief that a woman should not live vicariously through her spouse when they objected to allowing the wife of the president of the United States to deliver the commencement address. The official protest stated: "To honor Barbara Bush as commencement speaker is to honor a woman who has gained recognition through the achievements of her husband, which contradicts what we have been taught over our years at Wellesley." Those seniors may not have been fair to Barbara Bush, but they had learned the gist of Betty's message.

Noted for its political activity, NOW is today the largest women's-rights organization in this country. Among its current priorities is passage of the ERA, encouragement of women to run for political office, and publicizing issues such as pay equity, reproductive freedom, child care, and so on.

Attitudinal changes toward the women's movement have been significant. For instance, in 1971, 40 percent of women favored the women's movement; by 1986, 71 percent of all women believed that it had improved their lives. In 1966, only 5.9 percent of freshmen college women planned careers in male-dominated fields; 10 years later, this figure had increased to 19.4.

Writing for *Time* in 1989, Claudia Wallis said that many midcareer women blame the women's movement for emphasizing the wrong issues. The ERA and lesbian rights seemed to gain more attention than the need for child care and more flexible work schedules. She pointed out that many women are bitter because they put their careers first and at 40 find themselves childless. "Is it fair," she asks, "that 90% of male executives 40 and under are fathers but only 35% of their female counterparts have children?" Wallis also contended that nonprofessional women, poor women, and minority women feel that their needs and values have been neglected, that their primary concerns such as access to education, health care, and safe neighborhoods were not priorities for the women's movement. Last, she noted that stay-at-home mothers feel that their status has been deprecated by feminism.

But obviously women have made great advances. Here are some miscellaneous facts that reflect how their lives have changed since *The Feminine Mystique,* many of these changes attributable to the women's movement. Women born in 1900 could expect to be employed about six years of their lifespan of 46 years. In 1980, women were likely to be employed 29 years of their nearly 78-year life expectancy. The total fertility rate fell from 2.6 in the late sixties to 1.8 in 1976. The Supreme Court has legalized early abortion. It has also recognized sexual harassment on the job as a violation of Title VII of the 1964 Civil Rights Act. In 1983, 10.3 percent of the female population over age 14 was divorced, compared to 4.6 percent in 1960. Title 1V-D of the Social Security Act was amended in 1984 to enforce child support: states are required to garnish wages; the legal process is expedited; and collection methods enhanced. The Equal Credit Opportunity Act has prohibited discrimination on the basis of sex and marital status. Women have been included in the NASA astronaut program, the U.S. Coast Guard, police departments, fire departments, and other nontraditional areas such as construction, transportation, and engineering. The service academies are now integrated. There is equal representation of men and women at both Republican and Democratic National conventions. There has been an increase of women in the state legislatures (from 3 percent in 1971 to 14 percent in 1986). A woman was nominated for vice president on a major party ticket.

Marilyn French, the feminist author, has written this tribute to Betty Friedan: "She has been and remains a bridge between conservative and radical elements in feminism, and an ardent advocate of harmony and humane values."

Epilogue

It is interesting to examine some of the influences on the lives of the 11 women who are the subjects of this book.

The family backgrounds of these women were unusually good. Jane Addams was influenced by the example of her father's public spirit. Mary Bethune lacked material goods, but her parents were loving and ambitious for her. Juliette Low's mother may have been a difficult role model for her, but her father and brother provided support. Rachel Carson's interest in nature was fostered by her mother; on the other hand, for most of her life, Rachel was burdened with family responsibilities. Margaret Mitchell's passion for accurate detail about events in Georgia history could be traced to her father. While not all of these women were the products of higher education, they attained sufficient knowledge or skills to be successful in their endeavors.

Personal ambition is a driving force in many lives. The three Margarets—Mitchell, Bourke-White and Sanger—appear to have put considerable emphasis on their advancement, although Sanger's ambition was certainly intertwined with her cause. Addams, Wald, and Bethune were definitely ambitious, but they appear to have been driven more by altruism than desire for personal recognition.

Although religion is a motivating force for many, it did not seem especially important to the majority of these women. The exceptions are Mary Bethune and Juliette Low. Bethune declared publicly, "[God] is the Guide of all that I do. I seek Him earnestly for each need."

Probably because of the nature of their interests, Jane Addams, Lillian Wald, Mary Bethune, Margaret Sanger, Carrie Catt, Rachel Carson, and Betty Friedan regarded politics as a major concern. Apparently it was somewhat less important in the lives of Fannie Farmer, Juliette Low, Margaret Mitchell, and Margaret Bourke-White.

Native ability, exhibited in various forms, is a strong determinant for success. Jane Addams, Lillian Wald, Mary Bethune, Juliette Low, Margaret Sanger, Carrie Catt, Rachel Carson, and Betty Friedan were endowed with vision. Lillian Wald, Jane Addams, Mary Bethune, and Margaret Sanger demonstrated exceptional ability to raise funds in a period when people looked to philanthropy rather than government for financial assistance. Lillian Wald, Mary Bethune, and Carrie Catt were excellent organizers. Fannie Farmer, Margaret Mitchell, and Margaret Bourke-White were blessed with creative ability.

Progress usually requires perseverance, and all of these women—Mary Bethune, Margaret Sanger, Carrie Catt, and Margaret Bourke-White in particular—displayed it.

The times were right for some of these women. Immigrants captured the interest of Jane Addams and Lillian Wald. Mary Bethune saw the need to educate blacks in the Deep South. Carrie Catt was in a position to finish the cumulative work of many before her. Margaret Sanger was challenged by the restrictive atmosphere of the Comstock Act. Margaret Mitchell grew up at a time when the "Lost Cause" was still discussed frequently and at length. The discovery of DDT as an insecticide created the situation that Rachel Carson sought to end. Post–World War II attitudes about a wife's place being at home the contributed to Betty Friedan's resolution to make women less dependent. In contrast, Fannie Farmer might well have been making innovations in cookery a generation earlier or later. And surely Margaret Mitchell's imagination would have produced a masterpiece about any great movement that she experienced. War enhanced Margaret Bourke-White's fame as a photographer, but she probably would have excelled as a photographer in almost any situation. In fact, it is difficult to envision any of these 11 women as anything other than productive under circumstances different from those in which she found herself.

Personal courage is often a determinant in the realization of success. Jane Addams and especially Lillian Wald suffered because of their stand on pacifism during World War I. It required moral courage for Mary Bethune to promote civil rights in the hostile South. Likewise, Margaret Sanger, Carrie Catt, Rachel Carson, and Betty Friedan were courageous in their efforts on behalf of their respective causes, Margaret Sanger actually going to jail for her actions. Margaret Bourke-White exhibited a rare fearlessness during her war exploits. Fannie Farmer and Juliette Low displayed courage in overcoming their handicaps. Juliette, Fannie, Margaret Bourke-White, and Rachel Carson were exemplary in the way they accepted their final illnesses.

A woman's career is affected by marriage and children. Seven of the eleven women married. Six of them were divorced, producing collectively a total of only six children. Carrie Catt was married twice, apparently happily, but was also twice a widow and left no children. Margaret Bourke-White—twice married, twice divorced—recognized that her chosen path was not conducive to marriage and that it might have been different had she had children: "Perhaps I would have worked on children's books, rather than going to wars," she wrote in her autobiography. Sociologists have found that today women want and expect both career and family life just as men always have and as Betty Friedan advocated. But how that is going to be accomplished is far from resolved.

For the most part, these women were successful in obtaining their major goals, diverse as they were. However, Jane Addams and Lillian Wald were steadfast pacifists; Carrie Catt fought for peace after World War I; Margaret Sanger, Mary Bethune, Margaret Bourke-White, and Betty Friedan publicly advocated peace. Unfortunately they were not effective here. The United States was embroiled in World Wars I and II, the Korean conflict, and Vietnam. Some of the societal problems encountered by Jane Addams and Lillian Wald would continue for generations. Winning the vote for women did not automatically produce equality of the sexes, although it was a necessary start. Most feminists support ERA; Betty Friedan in particular worked for it assiduously, but it is not yet part of the Constitution. Jane Addams, in common with most social workers of her time, was a very strong supporter of Prohibition. Although she saw the Eighteenth Amendment ratified under President Wilson, she also witnessed its repeal under President Franklin Roosevelt.

In general, we may say that for these 11 women the common factors contributing to their success were talent and initiative; perhaps it would be preferable to refer to the latter as just plain gumption.

As seen at the beginning of the 1990s, the problems of the coming century presage unique difficulties. The United States will be fortunate indeed if it continues to be blessed with women of gumption who will find creative ways to solve these problems.

Selected Bibliography

Jane Addams

Addams, Jane. *Twenty Years at Hull-House*. New York: Macmillan, 1912.

Davis, Allen F. *American Heroine: The Life and Legend of Jane Addams*. New York: Oxford, 1973.

_____. *Spearheads for Reform: The Social Settlements and the Progressive Movement 1890–1940*. New York: Oxford, 1967.

_____, and McCree, Mary Lynn. *Eighty Years at Hull-House*. Chicago: Quadrangle, 1969.

Deegan, Mary Jo. *Jane Addams and the Men of the Chicago School, 1892–1918*. New Brunswick, N.J.: Transaction, 1988.

Farrell, John C. *Beloved Lady: A History of Jane Addams' Ideas on Reform and Peace*. Baltimore: Johns Hopkins Press, 1967.

Hull, Helen. *Unfinished Business*. New York: Macmillan, 1971.

Lasch, Christopher. *The Social Thought of Jane Addams*. Indianapolis: Bobbs-Merrill, 1965.

Levine, Daniel. *Jane Addams and the Liberal Tradition*. Madison, WI: State Historical Society of Wisconsin, 1971.

Linn, James Weber. *Jane Addams: A Biography*. New York: Appleton-Century, 1935.

Stead, William T. *If Christ Came to Chicago*. New York: Living Books, 1964 (originally published in 1894).

Fannie Farmer

Beeton, Isabella. *Beeton's Book of Household Management—A First Edition Facsimile*. New York: Farrar, Straus and Geroux, 1969 (originally published as a bound edition in 1861).

Bliss, Michael. *The Discovery of Insulin*. Chicago: University of Chicago Press, 1982.

Cunningham, Marion. *The Fannie Farmer Cookbook*, 13th ed. New York: Knopf, 1990.

Davis, Shelley. "Through the Years with the Cookbook of the Ages," *Washington Post,* Nov. 25, 1984.

Farmer, Fannie Merritt. *The Boston Cooking-School Book.* Boston: Little, Brown, 1921.

————. *The Boston Cooking-School Cook Book.* New York: New American Library, 1979 (a facsimile of the original, c. 1896).

————. *Food and Cookery for the Sick and Convalescent.* Boston: Little, Brown, 1907.

The Fanny Farmer Candy Shops, Inc. "A Short History of Miss Farmer and Fanny Farmer Candy Shops." Cleveland: no date.

Hartt, Mary Bronson. "Fannie Merritt Farmer: An Appreciation," *Woman's Home Companion,* Dec. 1915.

Hunt, Caroline H. *The Life of Ellen H. Richards.* Boston: Whitcomb and Barrows, 1912.

Lynes, Russell. In *The American Heritage Cookbook and Illustrated History of American Eating and Drinking.* New York: American Heritage, 1964.

Schlesinger, Elizabeth B. *Notable American Women,* vol. 1. Cambridge, MA: Harvard University Press (Belknap), 1974, 597–98.

Steele, Zulma. "Fannie Farmer and Her Cook Book," *American Mercury,* July 1944, 66–71.

Lillian Wald

Cross, Clare. *Lillian D. Wald: Progressive Activist.* New York: Feminist Press, 1989.

De Forest, Robert, and Veiller, Lawrence, eds. *The Tenement House Program.* New York: Macmillan, 1903.

Duffus, Robert Luther. *Lillian Wald, Neighbor and Crusader.* New York: Macmillan, 1938.

Hamilton, Diane. "The Cost of Caring: The Metropolitan Life Insurance Company's Visiting Nurse Service, 1909–1953," *Bull. Hist. of Med.,* vol. 63, #3, 1989, 414–35.

Siegel, Beatrice. *Lillian Wald of Henry Street.* New York: Macmillan, 1983.

Wagenknecht, Edward. *Daughters of the Covenant.* Amherst, MA: University of Massachusetts Press, 1983.

Wald, Lillian. *The House on Henry Street.* New York: Holt, 1915.

————. *Windows on Henry Street.* Boston: Little, Brown, 1934.

Mary McLeod Bethune

Brawley, James P. *Two Centuries of Methodist Concern: Bondage, Freedom and Education of Black People.* New York: Vantage, 1974.

Finkelstein, Louis, ed. *American Spiritual Autobiographies: Fifteen Self-Portraits.* New York: Harper, 1948.

Leffall, Dolores C., and Sims, Janet L. "Mary McLeod Bethune—The Educator; Also Including a Selected Annotated Bibliography," *Jour. Negro Education,* Summer 1976, 342–59.

National Education Association. *The Legacy of Mary McLeod Bethune.* Washington, D.C., 1974.

Juliette Low

Choate, Anne, and Ferris, Helen, eds. *Juliette Low and the Girl Scouts: The Story of an American Woman 1860–1927.* New York: Girl Scouts National Organization, 1928.

Dunphy, Owen. "March to the Sea," in *America's Civil War,* July 1990, 42–49.

Girl Scouts of the USA. *Facts about Girl Scouts of the USA.* New York, 1989.

Hillcourt, William, with Olave, Lady Baden-Powell. *Baden-Powell: Two Lives of a Hero.* New York: Putnam, 1964.

Howard, Jane. "For Juliette Gordon Low's Girls, a Sparkling Diamond Jubilee," *Smithsonian,* vol. 18, #7, 1987, 46–55.

Miller, Joni. "Scout's Honor: The New Uniform Is Blue," *Ms. Magazine,* March 1987, 58–59.

Rosenthal, Michael. *The Character Factory. Baden-Powell's Boy Scouts and the Imperatives of Empire.* New York: Pantheon, 1986.

Saxon, Martha. "The Best Girl Scout of Them All," *American Heritage,* vol. 33. #4, 1982, 36–47.

Schultz, Gladys Denny, and Lawrence, Daisy Gordon. *Lady from Savannah: The Life of Juliette Low.* Philadelphia: Lippincott, 1958.

Steese, Ellen. "Girl Scouts—75 Years Later," *Christian Science Monitor,* March 30, 1987.

Margaret Sanger

Broun, Heywood, and Leach, Margaret. *Anthony Comstock: Roundsman of the Lord.* New York: Boni, 1927.

Bylaws, Planned Parenthood Federation of America, Inc. New York, 1989.

Douglas, Emily T. *Margaret Sanger: Pioneer of the Future.* New York: Holt, 1970.

Drogin, Elasah. *Margaret Sanger: Father of Modern Society.* 3rd ed. New Hope, KY: Cul, 1986.

Gray, Madeline. *Margaret Sanger: A Biography of the Champion of Birth Control.* New York: Marek, 1979.

Kennedy, David. *Birth Control in America.* New Haven: Yale University Press, 1970.

Moore, Gloria, and Moore, Ronald. *Margaret Sanger and the Birth Control Movement: A Bibliography 1911–1984.* Metuchen, NJ: Scarecrow, 1986.

Sanger, Margaret. *My Fight for Birth Control.* New York: Farrar and Rinehart, 1931.

Sharman, Diana L. "Margaret Sanger: The Mother of Birth Control," *Planned Parenthood-World Population,* 1966 (reprinted from *Coronet*).

Valenza, Charles. "Was Margaret Sanger a Racist?" *Family Planning Perspectives,* vol. 17, #1, 1985, 44–46.

Carrie Chapman Catt

Catt, Carrie Chapman, and Shuler, Nettie Rogers. *Woman Suffrage and Politics: The Inner Story of the Suffrage Movement.* Seattle: University of Washington Press, 1923.

Fowler, Robert Booth. *Carrie Catt: Feminist Politician.* Boston: Northeastern University Press, 1986.

The League of Women Voters. "A Great Idea for Today: Facts." Washington, D.C., 1986.

Peck, Mary Gray. *Carrie Chapman Catt: A Biography.* New York: Wilson, 1944.

Kraditor, Aileen S. *The Ideas of the Woman Suffrage Movement 1890–1921.* New York: Columbia University Press, 1965.

Young, Louise M. *In the Public Interest: The League of Women Voters 1920–1970.* Westport, CT, 1989.

Margaret Mitchell

Edwards, Anne. *Road to Tara: The Life of Margaret Mitchell.* New Haven: Tichnor and Fields, 1983.

Farr, Finis. *Margaret Mitchell of Atlanta: The Author of "Gone with the Wind."* New York: Morrow, 1965.

Harwell, Richard, ed. *"Gone with the Wind" as Book and Film.* Columbia, SC: University of South Carolina Press, 1983.

Miers, Carl Schenck. *The General Who Marched to Hell: William Tecamseh Sherman and His March to Fame and Infancy.* New York: Knopf, 1951.

Mitchell, Margaret. *Gone with the Wind.* New York: Avon, 1973 (originally published in 1936 by Macmillan).

Pyron, Darden Asbury. *Recasting: "Gone with the Wind" in American Culture.* Miami, FL: University Presses of Florida, 1983.

Margaret Bourke-White

Bourke-White, Margaret. *Portrait of Myself.* New York: Simon and Schuster, 1963.
_____. *Shooting the Russian War.* New York: Simon and Schuster, 1942.
_____, with Jonathan Silverman, ed. *The Taste of War.* London: Century, 1985.
Brown, Theodore M. *Margaret Bourke-White, Photojournalist.* Ithaca, NY: Cornell University Press, 1972.
Callahan, Sean, ed. *The Photographs of Margaret Bourke-White.* New York: New York Graphics Society, 1972.
Goldberg, Vicki. *Margaret Bourke-White.* New York: Harper, 1986.
Rosenblum, Naomi. *A World History of Photography.* New York: Abbeville Press, 1984.
Silverman, Jonathan. *For the World to See: The Life of Margaret Bourke-White.* New York: Viking, 1983.
Time, special edition, "150 Years of Photojournalism," Fall 1989.

Rachel Carson

Brooks, Paul. *The House of Life: Rachel Carson at Work.* Boston: Houghton, Mifflin, 1972.
Carson, Rachel L. *The Sea Around Us.* New York: Oxford, 1951.
_____. *Silent Spring.* Boston: Houghton Mifflin, 1962.
Discover, special issue, "The Struggle to Save Our Planet," vol. 11, #4, 1990.
Gartner, Carol B. *Rachel Carson.* New York: Ungar, 1983.
Graham, Frank, Jr. *Since Silent Spring.* Boston: Houghton Mifflin, 1970.
Hynes, H. Patricia. *The Recurring Silent Spring.* New York: Permagon, 1989.

Betty Friedan

Blau, Justine. *Betty Friedan.* New York: Chelsea, 1990.
Chafetz, Janet Saltzman, and Dworkin, Anthony Gary. *Female Revolt: Women's Movements in World and Historical Perspective.* Totowa, NJ: Rowman and Allanheld, 1986.
Cohen, Marcia. *The Sisterhood: The True Story of the Women Who Changed the World.* New York: Simon and Schuster, 1988.
Friedan, Betty. *The Feminine Mystique.* New York: Norton, 1983 (originally published in 1963).
_____. *It Changed My Life: Writings on the Women's Movement.* New York: Norton, 1985 (originally published by Random House in 1976).

_____. *The Second Stage*. Rev. ed. New York: Summit Books, 1986 (originally published in 1981).

Major Accomplishments of the National Organization for Women and the Women's Movement. Washington, DC: NOW, 1986.

NOW Origins: A Chronology of NOW 1966–1985. Washington, DC: NOW, 1985.

Salter, Susan. *Contemporary Authors*. New Revision Series, vol. 18. Detroit: Gale Research, 1981.

Wallis, Claudia. "Onward, Women!" *Time*, vol. 134, #23, 1989.

Miscellaneous

Barck, Oscar Theodore, Jr., and Blake, Nelson Manfred. *Since 1900: A History of the United States in Our Times*. 5th ed. New York: Macmillan, 1974.

Cranden, Robert M. *Ministers of Reform: The Progressives' Achievement in American Civilization, 1889–1920*. Basic Books, 1982.

Flexner, Eleanor. *Century of Struggle: The Woman's Rights Movement in the United States*. Cambridge, MA: Harvard Univ. Press (Belknap), 1959.

Franklin, John Hope. *From Slavery to Freedom: A History of Negro Americans*. 5th ed. New York: Knopf, 1980.

Gruver, Rebecca B. *An American History*. Vols. 1, 2. 4th ed. New York: Newberry Award Records, 1985.

Harris, Mark Jonathan, et al. *The Homefront: America During World War II*. New York: Putnam, 1984.

Husock, Howard. "Fighting Poverty the Old-Fashioned Way." *Wilson Quarterly*, vol. 14, #2, 1990, 78–91.

Logan, Rayford W. *What the Negro Wants*. Chapel Hill, NC: University of North Carolina Press, 1944.

McHenry, Robert, ed. *Famous American Women: A Biographical Dictionary from Colonial Times to the Present*. New York: Dover, 1983 (originally published in 1980 as *Liberty's Women*).

McLaughlin, Steven D., et al., eds. *The Changing Lives of American Women*. Chapel Hill, NC: University of North Carolina Press, 1988.

Reed, James. *From Private Vice to Public Virtue: The Birth Control Movement and American Society Since 1930*. New York: Basic Books, 1978.

Rosen, Ellen Isreal. *Bitter Choices: Blue-Collar Women In and Out of Work*. Chicago: University of Chicago Press, 1987.

Rosen, George. *A History of Public Health*. New York: MD Pub., 1958.

Rothman, David J., and Rothman, Sheila M., eds. *Sources of the American Social Tradition*. New York: Basic Books, 1975.

Time, special edition. "Women: The Road Ahead." Fall 1990.

Index

Numbers in **boldface** refer to pages with photos

124130